CHILDREN OF ISLAM
A Teacher's Guide to Meeting the Needs of Muslim Pupils

Marie Parker-Jenkins
Foreword by Dr. Mirza Azam Baig

Research assistance by Kaye Haw

tb

Trentham Books

First published in 1995 by Trentham Books Limited

Trentham Books Limited
Westview House
734 London Road
Oakhill
Stoke-on-Trent
Staffordshire
England ST4 5NP

British Cataloguing in Publication Data
A catalogue record for this book is available from the British Library.

ISBN: 1 85856 034 9

Cover photographs:
With thanks to the children of Islamia Schools' Centre, London

Designed and typeset by Trentham Print Design Limited, Chester and printed in Great Britain by BPC Wheatons Ltd., Exeter.

Contents

Glossary of Terms

Akhira	Afterlife
Alema	female scholar of Islam
Ayaat	verses of Qur'an
burqa	cloak-like garment with veil
Hadith	reported traditions of the Prophet
halal	permitted
haram	forbidden
haya	modesty
hijab	covering, headscarf
Hajj	pilgrimage to Mecca
hubaya	long gown
Id ul Fitr	end of the fasting month of Ramadan
Id ul Adha	celebration of pilgrimage to Mecca
ilm	knowledge
Imam	leader of a Muslim community
izzat	honour
Jumu'ah	Friday congregational prayers
kameez	loose fitting top

madrassah	religious or mosque school
The Holy Qur'an	revealed book to Prophet Muhammad
Ramadan	the month of fasting
salat	daily prayers
Sharia	Islamic law
shalwar	loose fitting trousers
Sunnah	the deeds of Prophet Muhammad
ta'dib	education as conceived in Islam
tullab	seekers of knowledge
Ulema	male scholar of Islam
Ummah	Islamic community
wudu	ablution before prayer

Foreword

In the name of Allah, most Gracious, most Merciful

Today, when British Muslims are striving to achieve their basic human rights and establish an Islamic identity in this country, *Children of Islam: a teacher's guide to meeting the needs of Muslim pupils* is a welcome addition to the current debate. It encompasses the essential educational needs of Muslim children in a concerned and objective manner. Such an understanding is beneficial for both the majority and minority groups of the country, since it promotes co-operation and not confrontation. As the learned author has shown in her study, co-operation and mutual understanding between educators and the community has proved successful in achieving good results.

Children of Islam are citizens of this country and an appreciation and meeting of their educational needs is an investment in their future. Investment, in the form of provision of Muslim Voluntary Aided schools and the meeting of their Islamic needs in state schools, is actually an investment in this society. Surely future generations will benefit from such an investment.

Well educated Muslim children have a great deal to offer this society. A few Muslim schools who are struggling for their survival have won acclaim from educationalists, HMI, Secretaries of State and even a High

Court Judge. These poor schools, despite meagre resources of manpower and materials, are providing happy and healthy environments. Furthermore, these schools are offering training facilities for non-Muslim teachers from state schools and the ways and means of meeting the educational needs of Muslim children in the state schools. These children of Islam are surely a great asset for Britain. They are not a problem, as they are perceived in certain quarters of society.

These Muslim schools could prepare teachers for their future work in state schools. By twinning or having Muslim schools in the state sector, as suggested in this book, Muslim and non-Muslim schools can help each other. Muslim schools can offer Islamic education and Islamic ethos, while non-Muslim schools can offer training in school management and in-service education facilities to the Muslim teachers.

Dr Marie Parker-Jenkins, an enlightened educationalist, has been working and writing on Muslim children's needs for quite some time. This book is the result of her many years' painstaking work and research in Muslim and non-Muslim schools. The results of her research presenting contrasting views of Muslim and non-Muslim headteachers are interesting. I applaud her research and look forward to continued co-operation and understanding.

I hope that our educational administrators and political masters will take heed of this research so that the practical suggestions offered here may bear fruit for mutual benefits in society. Here is a chance to provide an example of putting theory into practice and creating beneficial co-operation between theorists and practitioners.

Dr Marie Parker-Jenkins presents her study in a well organised book. She gives the background of the children of Islam, the salient features of Islam and the basic principles of Islamic education in a very sympathetic manner. Each chapter ends with a brief summary which is very useful. The book has a comprehensive bibliography and a useful list of resources and contacts. In my humble opinion this book, *The Children of Islam* is a must for every teacher who, like myself, has in his/her care these children.

Dr Mirza Azam Baig
Principal, Islamia Schools
December 1994

Acknowledgements

The background research for my study of Islamic education began in 1989 when I approached a number of Muslim communities and schools. From visiting schools and interviewing headteachers, staff and pupils I obtained first hand information on Muslim schooling. Although I have refrained from naming individual schools for reasons of confidentiality, I would like to acknowledge their support here. The following schools have been gracious with their time, providing co-operation and assistance in my research:

Islamic Academy, Leicester
Islamia Schools' Centre, London
King Fahad Academy, London
Feversham College, Bradford
The Muslim College, London
Muslim Girls' School, Bolton

My study has also benefited from access to maintained schools which have, through their own experience of responding to the educational needs of Muslim children, developed important policy and practice. Particularly helpful were:

The Manning Comprehensive School, Nottingham
The Moat Community College, Leicester
St. Chad's C. E. Infant School, Derby
Arboretum Primary School, Derby

Rosehill Infant School, Derby
The Village Community School, Derby

I would like to express my gratitude to these schools, and to those which chose to remain anonymous.

Within my own institution, David Hay, Roger Murphy and Max Biddulph have given of their time in support of my work. I wish also to thank my research assistant, Kaye Haw for her meticulous efforts in the fieldwork and data analysis of the enquiry; and Jill Cleaver for her conscientious typing assistance. This was made possible financially, by a research grant from the University of Nottingham. In addition, on-going support throughout the past few years has been provided by Barrie Irving, Qamar Chaudhri, Aisha Desai and Freda Hussain, with whom I have enjoyed lively discussion about issues in this book.

Further afield, Muslim academics in the Faculties of Education and Theology in Marmara University, Istanbul and Nimat Barazangi of Cornell University, New York have been very helpful. Of particular support were Ahmet Sirin and Levent Deniz of Marmara University, who arranged for me to visit Muslim schools within their Islamic state, thus providing important alternative perspectives on educational policy and practice.

Finally, special thanks is due to Dr. Mirza Azam Baig who not only kept his school door open to me throughout the last five years but also graciously agreed to write the preface to this work. As a leading Muslim educationalist in Britain, I think he is particularly well placed to comment on the educational needs of Muslim children, to which he has dedicated his professional life.

While a number of educationalists and pupils have thus been consulted over issues contained within this book, the opinions expressed are attributable to myself; likewise any errors or omissions are my responsibility alone.

Marie Parker-Jenkins
University of Nottingham
October 1994

Introduction

What are the educational needs of Muslim children? How have some state schools managed to accommodate their needs, and in what ways can all academic institutions respond sensitively and sensibly?

Children of Islam seeks to answer these questions by drawing on theoretical and empirical perspectives. Based upon six years of research into the educational needs of this religious group, the discussion highlights the perceptions of both Muslim and non-Muslim headteachers. The purpose of the book is to explore these findings within the context of an accessible account of Islam. The discussion is aimed at educators and others interested in educational issues, who may have little or no knowledge of the religion. In addition to expanding knowledge of, and providing insights into the educational needs of Muslim children, the book is intended to have practical use. A glossary at the beginning contains key terminology associated with Islamic issues; examples of good practice are highlighted throughout the book; a needs analysis framework is provided to assist teachers measuring the accommodation of needs; and there is a list of resources for further information and for use in schools. Whilst the focus of the discussion is on Muslim children, many of the issues raised have application for other children within multicultural Britain.

The book is organised so that it can be read as a coherent whole or, alternatively, individual chapters provide self-contained units on themes pertinent to children of Islam. Beginning with an historical overview of Muslim communities in Britain, chapter 1 addresses issues concerning

statistics and differentiation; the establishment of mosques, denominational schooling, and the development of multiculturalism. The meaning
and significance of Islam and the attendant obligations on Muslim parents
and children are explored in chapter 2, followed by a discussion of Islam
and education in chapter 3, and the potential for conflict between secular
and Islamic philosophies of education. Chapter 4 describes the educational needs of Muslim children as portrayed by Islamic writers, and there
are practical suggestions for translating the theory into practice. In chapter
5 the discussion moves on to an empirical study exploring the views of
headteachers, both Muslim and non-Muslim, highlighting similarities and
divergence in their perceptions. These findings are discussed in greater
depth in chapter 6 and new categories of needs are developed which can
be used as a practical model against which to measure the extent of
accommodation, and as a move towards a hierarchy of needs which can
be tailored to the individual school situation. The book concludes by
locating the discussion in a broader context, raising political and philosophical concerns, and proposing a policy agenda for ensuring satisfactory
educational provision for Muslim children in Britain.

Chapter 1

Background

> The politics of difference ... aims for an understanding of group difference ... as entailing neither amorphous unity nor pure individuality (Young, 1990, p.171).

Muslim issues have become more prominent during the last decade. In the post-Rushdie era, and after the Gulf War and the Bosnian Crisis, social policy concerns have been highlighted, especially advocacy for the educational needs of Muslim children. Dissatisfaction over educational policy in the last decade has centred on: the difficulty of providing adequately for Muslim children in state schools; the call for public funding of Muslim schools; and the general concerns of Muslim parents who feel an incompatibility between values taught at home and at school[1]. This chapter provides background information on: (i) Muslims in Britain; (ii) the development of British education; and (iii) multiculturalism within a British context.

(i) Muslims in Britain

Muslims in Britain are by no means a homogeneous group. Here the focus is on settlement patterns; social differentiation; population statistics; sectarian differences and the role of mosques; and finally, the issue of 'fundamentalism'.

Settlement Patterns

Muslim immigration to Britain began from South-East Asia and regions of Africa in the 1940s. More recent migration can be characterised in terms of the 'pull' factors which attracted people to the country and the 'push' factors which forced them to leave their country of origin (Anwar, 1993, p.1). Economic growth in this country up to the 1970s and underemployment needs for manual, unskilled jobs constituted the pull factors, whilst higher unemployment rates and fewer economic opportunities were a significant feature of almost all the sending countries (ibid). The lack of immigration restrictions on people from New Commonwealth countries before 1962 facilitated an immigration pattern to Britain of wage-earners later followed by families; kinship and friendship networks resulted in a chain of migration contributing to concentrations in certain regions (Price, 1969). Pakistanis and Indians, for example, migrated to Britain in the 1960s and 1970s and maintained ideological and economic ties with their countries of origin (Watson, 1977). East African Asians arrived from Kenya in 1968 and Uganda in 1972 in sizeable numbers largely for political reasons (Hiro, 1973).

Settlement patterns of Muslims migrating to Britain meant that they were unevenly distributed. The majority are in the Greater London conurbation, the South-East, West Midlands, West Yorkshire, the South Lancashire region, and Central Clydeside, with Muslims frequently grouped together according to their country of origin[2]. Concentrations are to be found in major cities such as London, Bradford, Leicester and Nottingham. Settlement patterns have significance for the education system, especially in areas of large concentrations such as the recently established Bangladeshi community in Tower Hamlets, which requires provision from social services in general and specifically from schools.

The age profile of Muslim communities is also relevant. Thirty per cent of Muslims are of school age, compared with a general figure of 13%; and almost 60% of Muslims are under 25, compared to 32% nationally (British Muslims Monthly Survey, BMMS, 1993a). A further point on age breakdown relevant to this discussion is that 50.5% of Pakistanis were born in the UK compared with just over one third, 36.7%, of Bangladeshis (ibid). Bangladeshis were late migrants compared to other ethnic minority groups, and their dependents came later still. Clear implications for

2

schools regarding the educational needs of first and second generation Muslim children emerge here, and will be discussed in chapter 6.

'Muslim' and 'Asian' are not Synonymous

Muslims comprise the third largest religious minority in Britain today, after Roman Catholics and Anglicans (Ashraf, 1986 and Anwar, 1993, BMMS, 1993a). They are not however an homogeneous group; rather, the Muslim community in Britain is multiracial, multicultural and multilingual in nature and it is the faith dimension in their lives which provides a unifying characteristic. Hence it is more useful to perceive 'Muslim' as a generic term, encompassing people who are adherents to the same faith operating within Muslim *communities*, who differ markedly in cultural, linguistic and socio-economic features[3], and who have differentiated views on what Islam means to them and how it affects their lives. Furthermore, the word 'Muslim' cannot automatically be associated with 'Asian'. This is an important distinction to make since there is a misconception that Muslims in Britain are all of Asian origin. Likewise, not all Asians are Muslim; many embrace other religions, such as Hinduism, Sikhism or Christianity. This theme will be considered later but it is instructive to note here that, whilst Muslims share common beliefs, with a life-style based on the teachings of the Qur'an, they have diverse cultures and traditions. The generic label 'Muslim' conceals wide variations and the educational needs of Muslim children are directly related to these variations in religious background and cultural heritage.

None of the current 'labels' serve adequately to represent the various cultural or political identities of the millions of ethnic minority people in Britain. Moreover, a construction of ethnicity has been identified whereby 'a new cultural politics engages rather than suppresses *difference* and which depends, in part, on the cultural construction of new ethnic identities' (Hall, 1992, p.257). This concept of new ethnicities stems from the politics of ethnicity precluded on difference and diversity, set against the concept of 'Englishness' and disagreement over what it means to be 'British' (ibid). In this highly problematic and controversial area, self-designation is likely to be the only accurate descriptor, as provided within the 1991 Census. Furthermore, for the purpose of this work, the focus is on Muslims as a generic descriptor of religious affiliation, with the caveat of wide differentiation in linguistic, regional, cultural, political, and socio-economic backgrounds.

The Muslim Population in Britain

There are no definitive statistics on Muslims living in Britain. As official surveys do not ask questions pertaining to religious affiliation, estimates have to be drawn from questions relating to ethnicity. Using the 1991 Census and other statistical sources on demographic and social details, Anwar (1993) has attempted to calculate the number of Muslims in Britain. The recent survey was the first British census which included an ethnic question. It was based on nine categories: White, Black, Caribbean, Black Other, Indian, Pakistani, Bangladeshi, Chinese and 'Any Other' ethnic group. It is from this question on ethnicity, coupled with information on country of birth, that calculations can be made. The ethnicity question is useful in attempting to obtain a figure, because of the two categories of peoples originating from predominantly Muslim countries: Pakistan and Bangladesh. The majority of Muslims in Britain are from these countries and are sometimes described as visible minorities, easily identified by dress and skin colour. Speaking languages such as Gujerati, Urdu or Kutchi, these groups are further differentiated by regional affiliation, occupation, customs and traditions.

The data below indicates further that Muslims in Britain are not an homogeneous group. The main countries of origin are:

Pakistan	564,000
Bangladesh	164,000
Middle East	109,500
India	114,000
Kenya	71,100
Malaysia	27,000
Egypt	46,500
Libya	15,000
Morocco	13,600

(The Islamic Foundation, 1991)

Also included, but in much smaller numbers, are Muslims who are Greek or Turkish in origin. There are also Muslims from Indonesia, the Philippines and Singapore (Anwar). Hence the assumption that the word Muslim is synonymous with the term Asian is clearly erroneous.

Taking into account recent demographic trends, Anwar estimates that as of 1993, the Muslim population in Britain is approximately 1.5 million, and Sarwar (1994) calculates that around half a million are children of compulsory school age. In the absence of a question on religious affiliation in statistical surveys such as the Census, no exact figure is available and one and a half million can only be a working figure.

Sectarian Differences and the Role of Mosques

Among the one and a half million Muslims in Britain, there are variations based not only on national grounds but also on sectarian differences. The general public is probably aware of the Sunnis and Shi'ite sects among adherents to Islam, especially since recent events in the Middle East, but this over-simplifies the Muslim communities since there are other major sectarian divisions.

Raza (1993) provides a useful discussion of sectarianism among Muslims and the variety of groupings. He cites the major groups as: the Barelvis, to which the majority of British Muslims belong and which incorporates Sunnis; the Deobandis, a breakaway group of Sunni Muslims; the Tablighi Jamaat, based mainly in Dewsbury; the Ahl-e-Hadith, a large sect with a prominent centre in Birmingham; the Pervaizi based in London; the Jamaat-i-Islami, a much smaller number with Saudi Arabian connections; and finally, the Shi'ites, who originate from the Indo-Pakistani subcontinent and Iran[4]. As with other faith-based groups such as Catholics and Jews, these sectarian divisions incorporate strong differences in religious interpretation. Notwithstanding the concept of the *ummah* or united Islamic community, Raza describes the situation as one in which Muslims are divided by dissent and internal conflicts. In reality, the sectarian groups which form the Muslim communities in Britain differ on lines of politics, religious ethos and style of dress. Their interests are represented by mosques around the country, which announce their affiliation and provide religious and political representation.

The first mosque in Britain was founded in Woking in 1890 (Anwar, 1993). Many early mosques began in homes, and disused churches were converted where the Muslim concentrations settled. The role of mosques is varied: they may be 'a place of worship, a centre for education, judicial court and centre of government for administratives' (Alavi, 1989, p.6). It is calculated there are now over 1,000 in the country and the number is rising (Raza, 1993). Beyond leading religious services and providing educational instruction via a Madrassah or religious school, detailed in chapter 3, mosques form an important part of the political and sectarian life among Muslims. Indeed, it has been observed that 'the mosques in Britain have become a battleground for power politics'[5] and that:

> Mosque politics has a place of its own in the Muslim community ... an instrument of sectarianism ... As a focus of power the mosque is more powerful than Muslim organisations for it operates at grass root level (Raza, p.37).

At the centre of mosque politics are 'cultural, national sectarian, ethnic and class factors' (ibid).

Along with religious instruction and leadership, mosques form a vital role within the politics of everyday life in Britain. As the number of Muslims in this country increases so does their political awareness and politicisation. For example, the Muslim Manifesto, issued by the Muslim Institute in 1990, aims to set up a Council of British Muslims to act as a Muslim Parliament with representatives from Muslim youth and women (Raza, 1993). Part of their brief is to work to develop their own identity and culture within Britain, but as with other issues, Muslims are divided in their support of this organisation as they seek to identify and define their situation in this country.

There are implications for teachers. The local mosques in a school catchment area might serve a particular sectarian Muslim group and have very specific views on the range of issues which affect everyday school life. Given that they also play an important role in providing an educational programme for children, as discussed in chapter 3, there is clearly overlap in a) a dual provision of education for Muslim children and b) the potential for conflict or inconsistency between the two philosophies of education. Furthermore, there is no consensus among the mosques on aspects of education within the state school system, and questions of acceptable curricula, for example, will be influenced by the interpretation of Islam and views of *Imams* (leaders of a Muslim community) and *Alemas* (female scholars of Islam) in local mosques.

'Fundamentalism'

Mention should be made here of the term 'fundamentalism' since it is often pejoratively linked with the word 'Muslim'. The *Concise Oxford Dictionary* defines fundamentalism as:

> strict maintenance of traditional orthodox religious beliefs, such as the inerrancy of scripture and literal acceptance of the creeds as fundamentals of Protestant Christianity.

This definition could obviously be attached to a number of religious groups. Its origin, however, dates back to American Protestant churches and the establishment of the World Christian Fundamentalist Association (Yuval-Davis, 1992). Whether the term 'fundamentalism' has any application to Muslim communities is questionable however, since:

> some Muslim leaders have insisted that they are not fundamentalists, just devout Muslims. Others ... would apply the label to Muslims, but argue that one cannot put Christian and Muslim fundamentalists in the same category because of the different nature of the two religions (ibid, p.278).

Notwithstanding semantics and challenges on theological grounds, the term 'fundamentalism' has been applied in this instance within the context of anti-Muslim racism: as used by the media during and after the Rushdie affair, it has been used in the context of 'an abusive labelling of Muslims and their racialisation as the collective 'barbaric others'' (p.278). The term has further currency as a social phenomenon which cuts across other religions and cultures, particularly in relation to the position of women in society, and also in terms of religious superiority, whereby,

> the state privileges Christianity, which has put the issue of fundamentalism at the heart of the political debate. But different fundamentalist movements — Christian, Jewish, Sikh and Hindu as well as Muslim — have been growing in Britain during the past few years, partly as a result of international developments and partly as a result of the situation in Britain itself (p.278).

The term fundamentalism is thus employed in a manner consistent with other religious groups and with connotations which have significance and meaning specific to some Muslim groups in Britain. Fundamentalist movements can be perceived, therefore, as political movements with religious articulations; as liberation theologies or as militant causes[6]. Note also that, in Islam, fundamentalism has appeared as a return to the Qur'anic text (fundamentalism of the madrassa) and as a return to the religious law, the Sharia (p.280).

The rise in Islamic 'fundamentalism' has been linked with a fear of modernity which creates a lack of social moral order, and this encourages a return to religion as a source of comfort and identity. Certainly, the Rushdie affair produced in Britain 'a preoccupation with fundamentalist issues', thereby creating divisions with its focus on Muslims rather than fundamentalisms in all religions (ibid). Since Muslims in Britain are not an homogeneous body, the significance of fundamentalism within Muslim communities, if there is any, conveys different meanings: 'the role and meaning of fundamentalist Islam for second- generation Pakistanis who have grown up as a racial minority in the north of England, for example, are very different from its role for Iranians who have come to London as refugees' (p.279).

In short, the term 'fundamentalism' in its literal sense denotes a strict and narrow interpretation of theological texts and a return to spiritual guidance as a panacea against social ills. It also carries connotations of a patriarchal society controlling and oppressing women[7]. In that sense it clearly has relevance to other religions than Islam. From a Muslim perspective, the term has been used in a derogatory, racist manner during the Rushdie affair, and it continues to be employed pejoratively by certain media, fuelling a climate of specific anti-Muslim racism in Britain. Within Muslim communities, the term fundamentalism, where it has significance, is part of a return to spiritual values which help to explicate and reproduce religious identity.

To summarise: the term Muslim is not synonymous with Asian; followers of Islam in this country come from a variety of ethnic backgrounds. Most come from South-East Asia but there are also Muslims from non-Muslim countries and European converts. There is a danger of applying generic descriptors such as Pakistani, Bangladeshi or Indian, which conceal a rich variety of cultural and social-economic backgrounds within these categories. The diversity of backgrounds and socio-economic status needs to be understood and taken into account by teachers if an educational system responsive to needs is to be developed. Furthermore, there is the undeniable mixture of religion and culture within the Muslim child's background: where does one end and another start? Teachers are understandably confused by the different values and views held by Muslims on a variety of issues affecting school life, as evidenced in the Swann Report (1985), and as highlighted in this book. What is clear is that there is a shared Muslim faith but vastly different ways of following it: as in many faiths, religious adherence can be viewed on a continuum of orthodoxy to liberalism, involving both cultural heritage and patriar-chal arrangements.

For some Muslims who see themselves struggling to define their identity in Britain, the education system provides a focus for academic success but at the same time parents aspire to keep their children faithful to Islam. This generates discussion over educational provision in this country, within both the state system and the private sector.

(ii) The Development of Education in Britain

Educational provision in Britain was established on denominational lines dating back to the Middle Ages and faith-based groups have continued to perpetuate this tradition. By the 19th century, major social and economic upheaval due to the direct consequences of the Industrial Revolution[8] called for social policy enactment. Education was considered an important agent of social reform to assist the nation in its economic endeavours. Government at this time was, however, somewhat ambivalent about its role in the provision of educational services. Further, the Victorians were deeply suspicious of government involvement in daily events and feared the growth of state intervention into what had, hitherto, been a purely private concern[9].

Prior to 1850 what provision there was for educating the 'poorer classes'[10] was by virtue of the charity schools founded by such organisa-tions as the British and Foreign School Society of 1910 and the National Schools established in 1811. The origins of popular education in this country are ensconced in these charity schools, formed as a direct conse-quence of the 18th and 19th centuries' 'Age of Philanthropy'. Throughout Britain the clergy initiated schooling as a means of carrying out their evangelical crusade. *The Society for the Propagation of Christian Knowl-edge,* for example, attempted to recruit morally upstanding teachers, to assist in this mission. Similarly, teaching associations which flourished in the 1850s were often formed along religious lines, such as the Nottingham Churchmasters Association (Wardle, 1976). Whilst government began subsidising education to a limited degree in the form of treasury grants in 1833, it did not assume the role of instigator for educational provision, and universal free schooling was not implemented until the following century[11]. Instead, different faith groups were instrumental in promoting education with a strong inculcation of religious values and began a tradition in denominational schooling which has continued to the present day. Furthermore, when the state did choose to venture into providing education for all children, the clergy continued to have influence: indeed, education and Christianity were inextricably linked in the public mind (Tropp, 1957).

Denominational Schooling

Legislation enacted in 1902 and 1906 established the concept of a voluntary denominational school maintained by government funding existing alongside newly created board schools, the forerunner of local authority schools. Categories of denominational schools were designated in the *Education Act* (1944)[12] with various levels of government control but generally referred to as voluntary-aided schools. Most importantly for this discussion, the 1944 Act did not specify religious affiliation. The relevant clauses of the 1944 Act provide for different levels of support according to whether a school is classified as 'voluntary aided' or 'controlled', but they do not specify *which* denominational groups are to be included in the scheme. Hence, Jewish schools have been established through the procedure of obtaining voluntary aided status and Muslims, and potentially Sikh, Hindu and other minority groups, also wish to avail themselves of this right. Yuval-Davis sees Muslim 'fundamentalists' spearheading the campaign for separate schools but

> though Muslim fundamentalists are the most vocal, they are by no means the only groups demanding separate schools. Ultra-orthodox Jews, Seventh-Day Adventists, Sikhs and Hindus, have all done the same (p.286).

She adds that the Labour Party has embraced the calls for separate schools in the name of equal opportunities and anti- racism, but the Swann Report

10

concluded that voluntary aided Muslim schools would be socially and racially divisive.

The thorny issue in granting voluntary-aided status now to Muslim schools is that unlike previous denominations, this new group is perceived as predominantly of a visible minority. Racial segregation, as well as religious apartheid, appears to contradict government rhetoric on fostering multiculturalism. Notwithstanding the issue of 'voluntary apartheid' (NUT, 1984), as funding has not been forthcoming for minority faith groups, there is here an equality before the law issue[13]. Voluntary-aided status would bring with it grants towards capital costs of the buildings, and running costs and teachers' salaries would also be paid. If Muslim schools were afforded this status, they would be placed in the same category as the more than 7,000 Anglican and Catholic schools and 21 Jewish institutions which currently receive government funding of 100% running costs and 85% of capital costs (CRE 1990). Figures provided in 1991 by the Department of Education and Science (now the Department for Education) demonstrate that approximately one third of maintained schools fall within the voluntary-aided category and are denominational in character[14]. This accounts for 23% of all pupils educated within the state sector: there are 4,936 Church of England schools; 2,245 Roman Catholic; 31 Methodist; and 21 Jewish schools (ibid). Collectively,

> they represent a fudge and a mudge of religious and secular education, with the state paying the schools' running costs and 85% of their capital expenses, while governors and church leaders control the curriculum (Durham, 1989, p.12).

Private Muslim Schools

Private Muslim schools have tried unsuccessfully to be afforded voluntary aided status and to be in receipt of public funding. The most well-documented case of the Islamia School in Brent has been taken to the High Court and the government asked to reconsider its most recent rejection[15]. The new status would remove private Muslim schools from the jurisdiction of an unsympathetic local education authority and place them within the auspices of the national government which has traditionally made little interference in the running of such schools. Private Muslim schools which boast long waiting lists, have been increasingly clamouring for public funding along the lines of other denominational schools in Britain

(Halstead, 1986). Feversham College in Bradford (formerly the Muslim Girls' Community School) is another example of a school currently going through the relevant stages of the procedure, having obtained support from the local education authority which is experiencing a situation of lack of places for the children within its area[16]. In a policy statement on multicultural education, the opposition Labour Party signalled its general support regarding voluntary-aided status for Muslim schools (1989). Similarly, Baroness Cox unsuccessfully attempted to introduce the *Education Amendment Act* (1991)[17] which would have extended eligibility for public funding to independent schools providing an alternative religious ethos to existing state schools. More recently, the *Education Act* (1993)[18] contains provision for the government support of schools formed by voluntary groups. The door may yet be open therefore for Muslim schools to receive state finance.

The ideal environment to promote the Muslim identity and faith is believed by some to be within this separate school system. Muslims maintain that these are not intended to disunite society but to preserve their Islamic identity. The voluntary-aided or government financed Muslim school would thus be permeated by an Islamic ethos supporting their 'unshakeable faith' (Halstead). Muslim children, it is argued, would be better British citizens as a result of such schools, providing a moral compass, and instilling a new sense of morality into society.

Presently, there are approximately 25 independent Muslim schools in Britain which serve the needs of children whose parents are financially able and willing to pay[19]. The figure can only be given approximately for these institutions open and close randomly due to financial insecurity. In 1989 for example, the figure cited was 15 (Midgeley, 1989, Parker-Jenkins, 1991), and by the early 1990s the number given was in the area of 20 (Islamia, 1992a; Raza, 1993). They include a collection of single sex schools for girls and boys, primary and boarding schools (Rafferty, 1991; Midgeley, 1989). It is calculated that Muslim schools provide education for around 1% of an approximate population of 300,000-500,000 Muslim pupils in Britain (Weston, 1989; Berliner, 1993; Sarwar, 1994). It is from the approximately 25 Muslim schools in the country that a sample was selected for use in this book detailed later in chapter 5. Varying in number from approximately 5 to 1,800 on roll, Muslim schools coincide with the establishment of Muslim communities around the country, namely: the London, Leicester, Birmingham, Bradford, Kidderminster, Dewsbury areas. Relying on community support, they are seldom purpose-built and instead operate above a mosque or in disused schools, invariably connected to one or more mosques based on sectarian divisions, as mentioned earlier.

Muslim schools provide for parents who feel their children are caught in a situation of 'culture clash', whereby the whole ethos of British state schools and educational policy is seen as inconsistent with their way of life. Sarwar (1983) has highlighted the importance of cultural identity for Muslims and the fear that their community is threatened by the undermining of cultural consciousness. Since government supported Muslim schools are not yet a reality, as of 1994, there remains a basic problem; Muslim parents aspire to keep their children faithful in the face of perceived Western materialism and permissiveness.

Whilst some Muslim parents chose private schooling, in the absence of financial assistance from the government, others do not wish to see their children educated in ideological isolation and instead look to state schools to accommodate their needs. There is no coherent view among Muslim parents in this instance, as with those of other faiths, about the need for their children to attend a denominational school, or whether spiritual matters can be left to the family and attendance at religious services. Differences of opinion are highlighted by Taylor and Hegarty (1985), and the Swann Report (1985) cites Cypriot Muslims for example who are said to oppose separate schooling. Similarly, Bradford's first Asian Lord Mayor is quoted as saying:

> I don't want separation in any form ... what we want is accommodation of our cultural needs, especially in the education system (cited in Halstead, 1988, p.52).

This contrasts markedly with argument proffered by organisations like the Muslim Education Trust which suggests that there is a sizeable number of Muslim parents who do want government funding for separate schools (Cumper, 1990). For supporters of Muslim schools, the curriculum, both formal and hidden, should ideally reflect an Islamic orientation (Anwar, 1982; Hulmes, 1989). The significance of Islam and the importance of the Qur'an in education, as discussed in chapters 2 and 3, necessitate specific responsibilities of Muslim parents, and accordingly, certain rights and duties of their children.

There is also a different type of inadequacy and that is of provision. In the East End of London where Britain's largest Bangladeshi community is established, 'thousands of Muslim children were without school places in 1989 and 1990' (Yuval-Davis, 1992, p.286). Notwithstanding the governments legal obligation to provide schooling facilities and access to the National Curriculum, sizeable numbers of Muslim children have been denied their basic educational entitlement.

Single sex schooling is also part of the appeal for Muslim schools. Under section 36 of the *Education Act* (1944), it is the duty of the parent of every child of compulsory school age to cause him/her to receive efficient full-time education suitable to his/her age, ability and aptitude, either by attendance at school or otherwise. The term 'or otherwise' refers to home tutoring or education within the private sector. Instances have arisen where Muslim parents have failed to ensure their daughters attend school, because of an ideological opposition to co-educational schooling, and court proceedings have ensued (Barrell and Partington, 1985)[20]. Single sex education continues to be an aspiration for some Muslim parents, as discussed later in chapter 4, who see the phasing out of such schools as contrary to their interests. In Bradford, the Muslim Parents Association was formed in 1974 to represent the Muslim view on this issue and from this time a number of private Muslim schools were founded along single sex lines and in accordance with Islamic principles (ibid). More recently, Muslim schools for boys have been established to accommodate the wishes of Muslim communities who have expressed a need for single sex schooling for their sons as well as their daughters (Islamia, 1994). In the absence of schools promoting an Islamic faith, Muslim parents have opted for alternative denominational schools, such as those run on Anglican or Catholic lines which are seen to be supportive of both moral education and single sex schooling (Centre for the Study of Islam and Christian-Muslim Relations, 1985; Neilsen, 1987).

The issue of state funding for faith-based schools has generated debate in the 1990s, caused among other things by the decline in Christian intake and the clamouring for financial support for Muslim schools. Critical re-evaluation of the religious clauses of the 1944 Education Act with a view to dismantling all denominational schooling is a possible solution to the problem as raised in previous studies (Swann, 1985; CRE, 1990). This would clearly provoke angry responses from Anglicans, Roman Catholics and Jews who presently hold voluntary-aided status (Lustig, 1990). In the meantime, Muslim schools continue their struggle for equal access to the same funds and the vast majority of Muslim children look to the state school system for their needs to be accommodated. Diversity in society is reflected in the education system whereby 'multiculturalism' has attempted to respond to the reality of cultural pluralism.

(iii) Multiculturalism in Britain

Immigration after the second World War called for legal, political and social policy changes and the education system was not exempt from this process. Post-war immigration led to the increased presence of children from minority groups in the classroom and political ideologies were shaped in response to this reality. In education this took the form of six stages, frequently overlapping, whereby government attempted to respond to the reality of an increasingly multi-cultural, multi-lingual, multi-faith Britain.

Massey (1991) provides useful discussion of the key stages of government response to post-war immigration, commencing with one of *laissez-faire* or inaction:

> the assumption was that everyone was equal before the law, and therefore no special policies were necessary (p.9).

Accordingly, immigrants were expected to integrate into society after experiencing temporary difficulties. Racial tension in the late 1950s clearly highlighted the inadequacy and naivety of this ideological position and a phase of *assimilation* took place along with greater restriction of immigration to the country. Beginning in 1962 several Immigration Acts were passed limiting right of entry for those born in independent Commonwealth countries or colonies. In educational terms, assimilation via language and numbers took the form of introductory courses in English at infant and junior reception centres. Further, Department of Education and Science Circular 7/65[21] gave local education authorities permission for the dispersal or 'bussing' of immigrants where the quota of immigrants exceeded 33% of the school roll: 'justification for such a policy was educational, based on language development and a furtherance of cultural assimilation' (Massey, p.10). Milner (1983) highlights the fact that children were dispersed regardless of their length of stay in the country, whether language difficulties were experienced, and without parental consent. Assimilation and cultural re-socialisation were thus the avowed intent of the government as stated in the Commonwealth Immigrants Advisory Council report:

> if their parents were brought up in another culture or another tradition, children should be encouraged to respect it, but a national system [of education] cannot be expected to perpetuate the different values of immigrant groups (Massey, p.7).

Moreover, the assimilationist thrust assumed

> an obvious, definable homogeneous essence (the British culture) into which the hapless migrant might be inducted, given a suitable dose of English and an undiluted diet of the official school curriculum (Rattansi, 1992, p.15).

An ideological shift to *integration* as a concept next gained currency, sometimes presented, states Massey 'as a more sensitive development of assimilation' (p.11).

Social integration was predicated on grounds of linguistic integration, and bilingualism was seen as an impediment to this development. Section 11 funding introduced in 1966 helped support this policy, whereby local education authorities could claim back fifty percent of the cost of providing English as a second language from the Home Office and integration through compensation became a feature of this policy. Accordingly,

> language tuition itself was mainly confined to Asian pupils, and not extended to Afro-Caribbean children who were seen as speaking a deficient dialect of English which needed correction (Massey, p.11).

Cultures were thus valued according to how well they measured up to a normative concept which was white and middle class, and where they failed 'they were seen as deficient and inferior' (p.12). As problems of ethnic minority children were perceived as a result of cultural or linguistic deficiencies or its family structure, the school was not required to examine its role or teaching methodology of ethnic minority children; rather, policies and practices were presented in a deracialised form; and failure to integrate into British culture could be placed with the ethnic minorities themselves (ibid). Evidence of racial discrimination and alienation (Daniel, 1968) suggested that integration along these lines was unlikely to succeed or be acceptable, and education was seen yet again as an important agent of change in ameliorating the situation.

The development of *multiculturalism* denotes an important stage in the ideological shift away from the cultural imperatives of assimilation and integration to one of cultural pluralism. Generally acknowledged as originating in 1966 as a result of a speech by the then Home Secretary Roy Jenkins, the government called for the ideology of assimilation to be replaced by a policy of equal opportunity accompanied by cultural diversity. Multiculturalism was expressed in terms of creating tolerance for minority groups, dispelling ignorance, and reducing prejudice to create an harmonious society (Lynch, 1988; Jeffcoate, 1981). This phase can be summed up as one of equal opportunity in an atmosphere of mutual tolerance and cultural pluralism. Educational imperatives stemmed from evidence of underachievement (Rampton Report, 1981); civil disturbances (Scarman Report, 1981); and recommendations that there should be a shift to educating *all* children about living in multicultural Britain (Swann Report) thereby providing:

> legitimacy and impetus to local education authorities and schools already tentatively and sometimes vigorously pursuing one or another variety of multicultural and antiracist policy. ... it is arguable that Swann put multiculturalism and at least weak versions of antiracism on the national educational agenda (Rattansi, pp.12-13).

Schools responded by adapting a variety of approaches to teaching policy and practice. For example in the 1970s, Manchester adopted specific policies to tackle underachievement (Massey, p.14). Likewise, some education authorities such as Manchester, Brent, Bradford, Birmingham, East Sussex, and the now defunct Inner London Education Authority, issued guidelines on how schools could be responsive to the needs of Muslim children incorporating 'worthwhile initiatives and imaginative developments' (Sarwar, 1994, p.1).

The Select Committee on Race Relations and Immigration (1969) encouraged teaching about countries from which the minority ethnic children originated including art, songs and costume, leading to an approach to multicultural education in the 1970s caricatured as 'the 3 S

17

version — saris, samosas and steel bands' (Massey, p.13). Asian History and Caribbean Studies as non-examination courses were added to programmes of study, offered predominantly in multiracial schools:

> this kind of approach to multicultural education rested on the assumption that the poor performance and alienation in school of black and Asian children could be remedied by improving their self-images (p.13).

Government initiatives and documents endorsed this shift in ideology from assimilation to cultural pluralism thus:

> our society is a multicultural, multiracial one and the curriculum should reflect a sympathetic understanding of the different cultures and races that now make up our society (DES, 1977, para 10-11).

Adoption of a multiculturalist policy within education in the 1980s was accompanied by a plethora of texts on multicultural education, evidenced by the work of Craft and Bardell (1984); Jeffcoate (1981); Banks and Lynch (1986); Tomlinson (1984); and Troyna and Ball (1987) to name but a few. Critics of multiculturalism focused on the inadequate attempts of addressing cultural diversity through the curriculum; the reinforcing of stereotypes, superficial discussion of culture; the negative assumptions about minority children's sense of self-worth; attempts at social control; and the failure to confront racism both institutionally and personally (Troyna, 1986; Mullard, 1981; Troyna and Williams (1986). Furthermore,

> antiracists have pointed out that in privileging prejudice and attitudes the multiculturalists have neglected racism as embedded in structures and institutions (Rattansi, p.25).

The models within the umbrella term 'multiculturalism' were doomed to failure since they 'tinker with educational techniques and methods and leave unaltered the racist fabric of the education system'[22].

Beyond 'multiculturalism' lay a phase of anti-racist education in policy, provision and pedagogy (Troyna, 1986) aimed at challenging inequalities in society and schools. The two concepts multiculturalism and anti-racism both overlap and coincide within educational policy and practice. Connections were also made with inequality based on class and gender. Whilst there is overlap between the concepts,

anti-racism was seen as a radical departure from multicultural education, which was attempting to promote racial harmony on the basis of
understanding and appreciation of other cultures (Massey, p.17).

Moreover, the new model was seen as a radical political movement with
an emphasis on inequality and understanding of the roots of racism in the
economic and political systems. Anti-racism was conceived as being
instrumental in acknowledging and focusing on racism in society and
calling for schools to develop strategies to challenge and remove racist
practices. This manifested itself in local education authorities requiring
their schools to develop policy opposing racism and to implement
strategies aimed at tackling racist abuse and reviewing curriculum along
anti-racist lines. Berkshire and the ILEA for example, carried this out in
1983, followed by other authorities such as Birmingham and Bradford
(Massey).

Combining these two paradigms of multiculturalism and anti-racism
is what Massey feels constitutes the sixth stage which has application for
all schools. Indeed, Tomlinson (1990) notes the specific need of this type
of education in all white schools, which might be following a predominantly ethnocentric curriculum and assuming that multicultural education is irrelevant to the needs of their pupils. The synthesis of the two
paradigms demonstrates a greater awareness of racial injustice and
implementation of strategies to challenge and combat racism within the
school.

While the concepts of multiculturalism/anti-racism are subjected to
continual scrutiny and reappraisal, what multiculturalism has come to
mean to many Muslims, however, is that the liberal approach to multicultural education does not adequately address the convictions of the religious adherent: the secular has survived at the expense of the sacred
(Qureshi and Khan, 1989). It is perceived as an educational philosophy
seen as prompting Muslim children to scrutinise and challenge the authority of Islamic texts and authorities (Sarwar, 1983). Significantly, multi-
cultural/anti-racist teaching has been marginalised in some schools as the
implications of the *Education Reform Act* and local school management
became apparent in the early 1990s. The publication of the MacDonald
Report into the tragic events at Burnage High School has been widely
interpreted as signalling the failure of anti-racism within education
(Rattansi). At the same time Weldon (1989) has called for a return to an

integrationist policy, providing a set of British values to be embraced by everyone living in the country. Added to this, an ideological counter offensive from the New Right has led to a discernible lobby reacting against a perceived preoccupation with multicultural teaching, and instead invoking a doctrine of a common British citizenship. It would appear, therefore, that society has come full circle and is again contemplating a notion of assimilation.

Conclusion

In providing background information for the educational needs of Muslim children, this chapter focused upon three broad areas: (i) Muslims in Britain; (ii) the development of education; and (iii) multiculturalism within a British context. Of the one and a half million Muslims in Britain, it is apparent that there is no collective identity of those who adhere to Islam: rather Muslims are highly differentiated in terms of language, nationality, and socio-economic status. This is echoed in the work of mosques based on sectarian grounds. The diversity within the term 'Muslim' demonstrates that the word can only be used generically and self-ascribed identity within communities provides a more accurate nomenclature. Education policy and practice in the aftermath of immigration to respond to cultural pluralism resulted in a variety of ideological stances on a continuum from inaction, to assimilation, to multicultural/antiracism. None of these policies have proved entirely satisfactory and critics from both Left and Right of the political spectrum note the inadequacy in responding to the reality of multicultural, multilingual and multifaith Britain. In the meantime Muslim children, the majority of whom are in the state education system, are being educated in the post-ERA period in which multicultural/antiracist teaching has for many schools become somewhat marginalised. Notwithstanding the dilution of this educational philosophy of the late 1980s, some Muslim parents perceive educational provision in British state schools as a semisecular, Christian encounter in which Islamic faith and culture is undermined. In the absence of state funding for private Muslim schools, the situation remains that Muslim parents will aspire to keep their children faithful in the face of perceived Western materialism and conflict of cultural values. Those who remain within the state school system expect advocacy and accommodation of their needs, and enlightened educationalists who have some knowledge of Islam and the obligations which fall on Muslim parents and children, discussed in the next chapter.

Notes

1. I would like to acknowledge the work of research assistant Kaye Haw in conducting a literature review which helped inform aspects of this chapter.
2. South Asian Development Partnership (1992) *South Asian Population Report for Great Britain*, Sutton, Surrey: SADP.
3. With regard to social class, S. Castles (1984) *Here for Good*, London: Pluto, notes the lack of homogeneity among ethnic groups in general, and M. S. Raza (1993) provides interesting discussion of the need to see concepts pertaining to class, wealth and occupation from a non-Western perspective, in *Islam in Britain*, Leicester: Volcano Press Ltd., 1993, 2nd ed., ch.2.
4. For a further discussion of this theme see F. Robinson (1988) *Varieties of South Asian Islam*, Research Paper No.8, Centre for Ethnic Relations, University of Warwick.
5. The Islamic Cultural Centre, as cited in M. S. Raza (1993) *Islam in Britain*, Loughborough: Volcano Press Ltd., 2nd ed., p.37.
6. For more on these issues see A. Hyman (1985) *Muslim Fundamentalism*, London: The Institute for the Study of Culture, and J. I. Packer (1958) *Fundamentalism and the Word of God*, London: Inter-Varsity Fellowship.
7. Yuval-Davis (1992) develops this theme more fully in 'Fundamentalism, Multiculturalism and Women in Britain', in J. Donald and A. Rattansi, *Race, Culture and Difference*, London: Sage Publications, pp.278-291.
8. See A. Wood (1960) *Nineteenth Century Britain*, London: Longmans.
9. See S. J. Curtis and M. E. Boultwood (1966) *Introductory History of English Education since 1800*, 4th ed., London: University Tutorial Press.
10. These are defined in 19th century legislation as classes who support themselves by manual labour', and before 1870 the ability to pay school fees of 9d (4p) was a criterion in determining membership of the labouring classes. See Wardle (1976), *English Popular Education*, London: Cambridge Press, p.117 for more on this theme.
11. See W. H. G. Armytage (1964) *Four Hundred Years of English Education*, London: Cambridge University Press.
12. *Education Act* 1944, London: HMSO, ch.31.
13. I have highlighted this point of equality before the law elsewhere, see for example, M. Parker-Jenkins, (1993a) 'Muslim Rights', *Times Educational Supplement*, May 7, p.16, and M. Parker-Jenkins (1994) 'Playing Fair with Muslim Schools', *Guardian*, November 8, p.8.
14. Department for Education (1991) *The Parent's Charter: You and Your Child's Education*, London: HMSO.
15. The Islamia School in Brent went to appeal the government's refusal to grant it voluntary aided status in August 1993, and the High Court ruled that the government should reconsider the decision. See *British Muslims Monthly Survey*, 1993, 1(10), p.15. In light of voluntary aided status recently being given to a Jewish school, the

issue has become more contentious, see, 'Islamia and VA Status' (1994), *British Muslims Monthly Survey,* 2(8), p.20.

16. See Bradford Muslim Girls' School, *British Muslims Monthly Survey,* 2(6), 1994, pp.20-21; and 1(10), p.15.

17. *The Education Amendment* 1991, London: HMSO, Bill 8, HL.

18. The Education Act 1993, London: HMSO, part vi, section 229- 230. See also, G. Walford (1994) 'The New Religious Grant-Maintained Schools', *Educational Management and Administration,* 22(2), pp.123-130.

19. Information and data for this section is drawn from my research into Muslim schools in Britain conducted since 1989, involving visits to 25% of these institutions to see at first hand educational provision, and to explore issues of concern.

20. See for example a recent case of a Muslim father who successfully appealed against his daughter having to attend a mixed secondary school in Hull, *British Muslims Monthly Survey,* 1993, 1(9), p.10.

21. Department of Education and Science, (1965) 'The Education of Immigrants', *Circular 7/65,* London: DES.

22. Institute of Race Relations (1980) as cited in I. Massey (1991) *More Than Skin Deep,* London: Hodder and Stoughton, p.15.

Chapter 2

Islam: Relevance and Meaning

> Allah has conferred a favour upon you that He has guided you to the Faith, if ye be true and sincere (Qur'an, 49:17).

Beyond religious events such as Ramadan, what do teachers generally know about Islam? This question raises serious and important issues about knowledge and understanding of Muslim pupils and the role of faith. In examining the meaning and relevance of the Islamic faith to its adherents, this chapter focuses on (i) Islamic values; (ii) the development of an Islamic consciousness; (iii) the role of the mosques; (iv) and the obligations placed on parents and children in practising their faith. Particular emphasis is placed on the influence of faith in governing and shaping everyday life and the implications for educationalists.

Islam is not simply the name of a world-wide religion but rather an all-embracing way of life with submission to the faith, constantly reaffirmed through personal behaviour[1]. Submission to God or Allah, and adherence to religious principles is considered both a duty and a privilege leading to inner harmony and peace, and happiness in the hereafter or the next life:

Islam is a complete way of life. It is the guidance provided by Allah, the Creator of the Universe, for all mankind. It covers all the things people do in their lifetime. it shows us the best way to conduct our private, social, political, economic, moral and spiritual affairs (Sarwar, 1992, p.13).

There are two central meanings of Islam, therefore, submission to God and the acquisition of peace: quite literally the word 'Muslim' in Arabic means 'one who through submission to God enters into peace' (Hulmes, 1989, p.31). There are impressive figures world-wide demonstrating that Islam is a rapidly growing faith and in Britain the religious group represents the third largest religious minority in the country (Ashraf, 1986)[2].

Muslims are provided with guidance on all aspects of life through religious texts and community interpretation of the holy scriptures. Originally written in Arabic, the Qur'an is the holy book of Islam containing 114 chapters (or surahs) and 6,236 verses (or Ayaat), which God or Allah revealed to the Prophet Muhammad in the seventh century AD (Sarwar). The Qur'an is respected by Muslims as a book of authority and a source of law in Islam, and the Islamic principles contained within it are said during community and individual prayer time (Sarwar). The word 'Qur'an' means 'that which is recited or read aloud' and the symbol of a committed Muslim is the ability to recite the entire book, thus achieving the status of a hafiz (male) or a hafiza (female). The Qur'an is invoked for guidance by Muslims in all matters and many followers of Islam aspire to learn Arabic so they can read and recite it in the original rather than rely on vernacular translations. Furthermore, the significance of the Qur'an is that it imparts principles of guidance which are passed on from generation to generation.

It is from the Qur'an that the words 'Islam' and 'Muslim' are used: 'the religion before Allah is Islam' (3:19); and 'He named you Muslims before and in this' (2:78). Finally, Islam has five basic duties which practising Muslims must perform, known as 'the five pillars of Islam'.[3] Highlighted in the Hadith, or sayings of the Prophet Muhammad, they are:

Shahadah — declaration of faith
Salah — five compulsory daily prayers
Zakah — welfare contribution

Hajj— pilgrimage to Makkah

Sawm— fasting during Ramadan (Sarwar, 1992 p.41).

Islam is centred upon these five bases: declaring that there is no god but Allah; that Muhammad is Allah's messenger; the establishment of daily prayers; the payment of zakah and fasting during the month of Ramadan. With perhaps the exception of zakah or welfare contribution, these pillars of the faith will affect Muslim children throughout the school year, especially beyond the age of puberty, and salah or compulsory daily prayers has particular implications for schools, as explored later in chapter 4. Here, it must be stated that the ritualistic following of the five pillars does not by itself make a Muslim. Rather, knowledge and understanding of Islamic values and translating them into everyday life is equally part of what it is to be a true Muslim (Sarwar, Ashraf).

(i) Islamic Values and Attitudes

Inherent within these Islamic principles are values and qualities which help to shape the Muslim consciousness:

> The goal of Islam — of its concepts, worships and teachings relating to values, attitudes and behaviour — is to create an Islamic personality within the Muslim individual (Haneef, 1979, p.63).

Such a personality rejects the supposition that there exists nothing but the material world and instead lives with the certainty that a divine God is responsible for all creation and to whom one is accountable:

> the commitment is total and extensive. He acknowledges his dependence on this Being, accepts His laws as the rules which guide his life, and surrenders himself to Him. He is always conscious of God, remembering Him in all his activities and concerns. Islamic values and attitudes are the base on which his personality is built and Islamic criteria govern all aspects of his life (ibid).

Islam's central concept, as stated earlier, is faith in and submission to God, and collectively Muslims form an Islamic society obedient to God's commands, confident they will be rewarded in the *Akhirah* or Hereafter. Often referred to as the *ummah*, the Muslim community ideally unites behind the banner of Islam, abandoning all national and sectarian divisions:

> Differences in customs and conventions of different regions do not mitigate against this sense of unity ... As Islam is a complete code of life, Muslims all over the world are expected to follow the same code. Local customs and ceremonies differ but the basic principles and practices are the same (Ashraf, 1993, p.3).

The Arabic word *ummah* conveys this idea of an Islamic community which is unified and to which loyalty is due:

> a clear line of division exists between those who are members of the community and those who are not. But this exclusiveness is not necessarily permanent. No one is excluded from the Islamic community on grounds of race or colour. Individuals exclude themselves by not accepting the claims of Islam' (Hulmes, p.32).

The preservation and health of the *ummah* is considered an important aspect of the faith and 'depends upon the success which Muslims have in protecting the community from the danger of alien elements' (ibid, p.33). The employment of energies and resources to establish an Islamic system of life in order to please God is known as *Jihad,* from the Arabic 'to try one's utmost' (Sarwar, p.81). The Jihad is within the individual, a continuous process to establish right or *Ma'ruf* and to remove evil or *Munkar* from individual lives and society in general:

> we must carry out our duty to do good ourselves and urge others to do the same. This will enable us to remove our weaknesses and deficiencies. None of us is perfect, but our imperfections will gradually decrease if we do our very best to pursue our duty of Jihad (ibid, pp.81-82).

Two important issues emerge for educationalists from the discussion so far: firstly, community views and involvement is focused on preserving the tenets of Islam which form an important part of everyday life. Muslim families may perceive their life within the context of the *ummah* or community, rather than as an independent nuclear or single unit. Furthermore, reaction from the community over dress, behaviour or un-Islamic conduct is likely to be taken seriously by parents and children. Secondly, the local ummah is likely to concern itself with matters relating to education and its consistency with Islam. Legitimisation of educational policy and practice by the local ummah and its Imams will assist Muslim parents in feeling comfortable with the state schools and their children's progress within the education system.

(ii) The Development of an Islamic Consciousness

Islam has a strong influencing factor on matters pertaining to everyday life, governing human behaviour and conduct. Nowhere is this more important than in the relations between the sexes. Islamic society is governed by both individual and collective responsibility and the religious texts of Islam set limits for human behaviour. Based on general guidelines, 'Islam has established certain principles to govern the interaction of the sexes and control sexual behaviour among Muslims' (Haneef, p.155). Casual social interaction of the sexes is not permitted: where it does take place, it is only encouraged for serious, legitimate purposes and throughout the Islamic world, schools and public facilities have frequently been established on a single-sex basis. For some Muslims, segregation of the sexes also exists when entertaining in the home (ibid). Neither do females attend the mosque in some Muslim communities: rather, the duty to pray is seen as a domestic activity, although this tradition is being challenged (Darsh and Lemu, 1992). Further, where mixing does takes place 'both men and women are to exercise propriety in the way they speak, look and behave' (ibid). This also applies to individual dress and for some adherents to the faith:

> the Muslim woman is required to conceal her attraction from men by a strictly modest, straightforward type of attire (p.156).

This may extend beyond the home, especially

> outside her home and at any time when she is in the presence of non-*Mahrem* (non-relatives) ... she is required to wear a covering-type of dress which will make it clear to anyone who sees her that she is a chaste, modest and pure woman (ibid).

The extent to which Muslim women should cover themselves is debatable and Muslims themselves are divided over this, often differentiating themselves on cultural as well as religious grounds. Individuals choose the degree to which their Muslim identity is symbolised and apparent within society and,

> For Muslim women the issue of multiple worlds is more pronounced than it is for men because of the issue of dress and visibility. Dress whether one identifies with it as an issue or not, has a subconsciously powerful impact (Hermansen, 1991 p.193).

Some Muslim women challenge the legitimacy of covering their heads, for example, and maintain that the stipulation has more to do with patriarchal and cultural traditions, rather than strict Qur'anic interpretation[4]. For the purpose of schools in Britain, however, some Muslim families may feel very strongly about what is considered an acceptable dress code and this is explored in further detail in chapter 4 within the context of school uniform. What this does raise, however, which is of importance here, is that religion is a cultural expression as well as a religious belief: it is difficult to determine where one ends and the other begins. Hence behaviour and belief among Muslims about a variety of issues can originate from cultural tradition and heritage rather than strict Qur'anic interpretation. Further, some Muslim parents may experience anxiety and difficulty in attempting to preserve what they interpret to be cherished Islamic principles within a non-Islamic society and school system.

Modesty in dress, manner and behaviour by virtue of Islamic guidelines applies to males as well as females for Islamic teachings inculcate in both sexes 'a strong sense of *haya*', that is 'shyness, reserve and modesty in the presence of the opposite sex' (Haneef, p.157). For a Muslim woman, her modesty, dignity, piety, intelligence, and role as wife and mother 'are the sources of status and respect within the community' (ibid). There are clear implications here about the appropriateness of dress, and the display of behaviour which is not in the genre of *haya* or modesty and shyness. Very importantly, Muslim children are taught to respect and not question elders or those in authority and accordingly they may appear to be stereotypically passive and accepting. If a child does not question teachers it does not automatically denote lack of interest or intelligence but rather respect for their authority and position. Furthermore, the value placed on deference to authority, and *haya* or modesty within the Islamic consciousness, helps to explain the difficulties and contradictions some Muslim children may experience in participating in state school activities which call for assertiveness and extrovert behaviour. This also raises implications for the way in which certain lessons such as physical and sex education classes are taught in schools. The content and methodology of these aspects of the curriculum are explored further in chapter 4, but for the purpose of this discussion Islamic attitudes on mixing between the sexes suggest that:

> Muslims generally do not feel at ease with the current trends in Western society ... [they] are often deeply shocked by the general lack of shame and modesty, by the fact that illicit sex is no longer censured in the society as a whole (ibid).

The avoidance of bringing dishonour to the family is something Muslim children have instilled in them from an early age but this is particularly enforced around the age of adolescence. Behaviour between the sexes raises important issues for conduct between teachers and parents:

> to a conscious Muslim man or woman, attention from any member of the opposite sex other than one's own spouse in the forms of free talk, compliments, playfulness, suggestive comments, touching in any form (including handshaking and patting on the back), and anything else which has sexual undertones is insulting, degrading and very much disliked (p.158).

Clearly, it is quite possible to cause offence unintentionally through, for example, non-verbal communication which non-Muslim educators may use to extend greetings and hospitality at parent-school functions.

(iii) The Role of Mosques in Islam

The role of the mosques in the life of Muslims is multi-faceted, as outlined in the previous chapter, but for the purpose of this discussion it is important to note the significance of mosques and imams in relation to the Islamic faith. Mosques serve the community as religious institutions for public prayers, in addition to other functions, and after the home and work it is the most frequented place for Muslims. The word *mosque* is derived from the Arabic *masjid* which literally means a 'place of prostration' where public prayers takes place. The Imam or leader of the local Muslim community is normally a person of exemplary reputation and

29

character who acts as a teacher and a judge in matters of dispute. From the word in Arabic, *imam* means one who stands before or in front of the community for public prayer purposes to lead the religious proceedings (Sarwar). The imam is likely to be approached for guidance and clarification on matters of everyday life and this includes educational issues. Some state schools, as discussed later in chapter 4, establish contact with the imams of their local Muslim communities and make use of their services for religious guidance and school governance. Consultation with local imams can assist schools in understanding key issues of importance in a child's upbringing and in attempting to avoid misunderstanding. Different mosques will hold different views about what is or is not acceptable pertaining to children's education. Accordingly, to understand and assist in meeting the educational needs of Muslim children, educators need to understand the local mosque community from which their pupils are drawn.

Associated with mosques are religious or mosque schools called *madrassahs*. Areas around the country which are densely populated by Muslims provide a variety of supplementary schools or madrassahs for teaching the Qur'an in the evenings or weekends (McLean, 1985). If the mosque is some distance from where the children live, the community is encouraged to make arrangements for classes to be held in someone's home on a regular basis and, if necessary, obtain the services of peripatetic teachers with the necessary religious training (Ashraf, 1993). It is estimated that approximately 90% of all Muslim children between the ages of 5 and 12 attend such schools at some time (Hussain, 1990). Therefore, in addition to attending compulsory education in the day, many Muslim children will be learning Arabic in order to read and understand the Qur'an and Islamic principles. It has been stated that the obligation to attend a madrassah occurs 'one or two evenings each week' (Hulmes, 1989) although from the author's research this activity was found to be double that commitment in terms of time. This raises questions about when and where homework from day schools is taking place. Content and methodology of teaching in madrassahs are discussed further in the next chapter, but an important issue to note here is the obligation placed on a Muslim child to attend supplementary education for religious purposes. Clearly, Muslim children's obligation to attend a madrassah and receive compulsory education from the local authority school or alternative provision, means that their working and learning day is considerably longer than that of their non-Muslim counterparts.

(iv) The Role and Duties of Parents

[Muslims] will try to find ways of educating their children so that the distinctive claims of Islam are fully recognised (Haneef, p.33).

The traditional interpreters and transmitters of Islamic values and attitudes are the parents whose responsibility to do so begins at the time of a child's birth:

long before children are able to understand the meaning of the words, their mothers whisper to them the basic creed of a Muslim: 'There is no god but Allah ... and Muhammad is the messenger of God' (ibid, p.39).

The obligation to ensure that a child is brought up according to Islamic principles is a responsibility of the entire *ummah* or community, 'but for the parents and the immediate family this is both a duty and a great privilege' (ibid, p.37). There is a fear that they may be thwarted in their attempts and that perceived Western secular views will undermine this effort:

the ideas, ideals and fruits of western expertise are, intentionally or not, the instruments of cultural imperialism in various subtle ways. And all are potentially subversive of Islamic values (ibid, p.38).

Furthermore,

religion does not form the basis of modern education. Neutrality, rather than apathy, to religion is the dominant principle adopted by curricular designers ... Thus children and youth have to depend on their parents for initiation into religion, for the maintenance of religious principles and practices and for the preservation and furtherance of the Islamic way of life (Ashraf, 1993, p.3-4).

The fear that their religion will be undermined and that their young will abandon the faith is of course shared with other groups[6]. Muslim parents aspire to keep their children faithful in the face of perceived decadence and conflict in values and attitudes about everyday life. Writing about

31

Asian Muslims specifically, Modood (1992) notes the relevance of family background and inherited norms and values:

> there is now considerable and growing evidence that on a whole range of issues to do with sex, gender roles, arranged marriage, mixed marriages, female dress, family authority and honour, extended family and preservation of cultural identity, second generation attitudes are closer to their peers in the sub- continent, than to their British peers (pp.263-264).

In order to reduce the potential for conflict in values, parents are expected to ensure that 'a monocultural programme' is provided whereby the child's background, religion and identity is affirmed: only then can parents contemplate moving onto a multicultural education for their children (Ashraf, p.11). There is thus a twin role played by both the community and parents to see that children get habituated to prayer and recitation of the Qur'an from childhood and the co-operation of the parents is seen as essential in this endeavour (ibid).

The significance of Islam in their lives and the importance of the Qur'an for their religious education require specific responsibilities of Muslim parents, and accordingly, certain rights and duties of their children. Further:

> among Muslims children are very much loved and wanted, a precious gift and trust from God ... Parenthood is regarded as desirable and rewarding (Haneef, p.148).

Muslim children are expected to respect and obey their parents as commanded in Qur'anic verses, such as 'do good to parents' (6:151). Muslim families are normally very close both emotionally and physically and often surrounded by a wide circle of members of the extended family. Guidance and training of Muslim children begins very early:

> their goal is the moulding of the child into a sound Islamic personality, with a good character and morals, strong Islamic principles, sound Islamic knowledge, proper Islamic behaviour, and the equipment to handle the demands of life in a responsible and mature fashion (Haneef, p.150).

The training of children into a religious ideology is consistent with other faith-based groups in society. What is noteworthy, however, is the early

32

age at which Muslim children begin training and accept moral responsibility. By the age of five or six, the average Muslim child will have some knowledge of creation and the forces of good and evil, because this forms:

> a vital part of his consciousness and comprehension of reality as he grows up ... hence a sound conscience is developed early, and at a young age he is capable of being the watcher over his own actions (ibid).

Responsibility for personal behaviour is also instilled at a very early age:

> Muslim youngsters are considered by Islam as accountable to God for their own actions by the time they attain puberty (ibid, p.151).

Conscientious Muslim teenagers are expected to stay away from what is known to be prohibited or harmful and to prepare for their future roles in adult life. Clearly, there may be activities concerning school or British life in general, which are problematic for Muslim teenagers attempting to fulfil their Islamic obligations and also negotiate their way in a manner acceptable to society in general.

To accomplish the overall goal of nurturing a child as a Muslim and in the Islamic way of life, parents are expected to set an example personally,

> conscientious Muslims do their best to avoid behaviour, activities and companions which do not fit in with a pure Islamic life (p.150).

Obedience, respect and consideration for parents is also encouraged, as summed up in the Muslim proverb:

> the pleasure of God is the pleasure of the parents (ibid).

As noted earlier, deference to parents and teachers, rather than challenging authority figures, is part of Islamic education which may appear at odds with the educational philosophy within the state school system, where deference to authority is not always expected or encouraged. Furthermore, where education is concerned:

> they see to it that their child has proper instruction in the teachings of Islam and encourage him to fulfil his obligations; they place him (insofar as they have any choice in the matter) in a school situation which is good for his total education, and are careful about ... what he is permitted to do (pp.150-151).

In short, Muslim parents are expected to ensure their children have a complete training in Islamic principles, concepts, values, attitudes, morals and behaviour. This takes place firstly in the home where the parent is the initial educator; and secondly through supplementary education in *madrassahs*. Furthermore, the ummah or Muslim community expects parents to take this role seriously, of inculcating Islamic principles and values into their children, and to be seen to be doing so by the way they involve themselves in their child's religious and secular education.

Having raised their young along sacred Islamic lines, the relationship between parent and child continues beyond careers and marriage:

> ... while there is a natural branching off when a young man forms his own home with his wife or a girl goes to the home of her husband, the parents are not replaced in their affection by the newly-formed relationship ... parents and children remain part of a single family unit whose members are bound together by the strongest ties of duty and affection (p.152).

This bond continues into old age in keeping with Qur'anic dictates:

> in general 'we have enjoined on men kindness to parents' (29:8) and later in life: 'address them in terms of honour, and out of kindness, lower to them thy wing of humility and say, 'My Lord, bestow mercy on them as they cherished me in childhood' (17:23:24).

Such behaviour and treatment between parent and child is expected to serve as an example and inspire future generations. Furthermore,

> the duty of their children does not end with the death of the parents, for they continue to mention them in their prayers and to make supplication for God's mercy on them until the end of their lives (Haneef, p.155).

Thus the bond between parent and child, and deference to parental authority continues as a significant feature of the Muslim family.

Finally, the obligation placed on Muslim parents is active not passive: duties are such that they must be seen to be bringing up their children in the Islamic way of life. Clearly, this can involve making demands of schools over issues such as dress, diet and prayer — as discussed later in chapter 4. Parental involvement in their child's education is underpinned by legislation, both British and European, which provides for schools to respect the religious and philosophical convictions of parents with regard to their children's education[7]. Increasingly parents of all groups, religious or not, have been encouraged by recent legislation to become more active in their child's education: where the child has a religious background, this may require specific accommodation by schools.

Conclusion

To summarise this chapter on 'Islam: relevance and meaning', Muslims take their religion to be all-encompassing, affecting everyday activities. Islam totally rejects the supposition that there is no Afterlife, and instead requires followers to ensure that their behaviour, values and attitudes, are consistent with principles detailed in the Qur'an and *Hadith*. The religion is perceived not only as a moral code but as a bulwark against modern atheistic concepts[8]. Based around the concept of the ummah, Muslims aspire to keep themselves and their young faithful through guidance and training at home and through supplementary schools or madrassahs. Although Muslim communities are perceived by some as cores of resist-ance in liberal democracies, and pejoratively labelled by some elements of the media as 'fundamentalists'[9], they see themselves as carrying on the basic tenets of their faith and resisting the tide of secularisation within both society and schools. Education begins in the home before formal education in school and parents see their role in this matter as one of duty and privilege to ensure their children develop an Islamic consciousness. The demands of imams, and parents to schools are seen as a crucial attempt to ensure that their religious identity is not undermined and that Islamic values are fostered among the young.

It is an over-simplification, however, to suggest that Islam holds the same central focus for all Muslim children. Rather, Islam plays a complex and differentiated role for its adherents and alternative interpretations on what it means to be a Muslim will affect everyday life-styles differently. All of this clearly has implications for educationalists in terms of educa-tion policy and practice, and curriculum content and methodology, ex-plored in subsequent chapters. Before that, however, it is useful to broaden this discussion from the relevance and meaning of Islam, and examine the relationship between Islam and education, explored in the following chapter.

Notes

1. I would like to acknowledge the kind assistance of Qamar Chaudhri and Asaf Hussain in reading this chapter and checking for accuracy in the interpretation of Islam and Islamic principles.

2 British converts to Islam have recently been reported to be in the region of 10,000 with a major proportion consisting of females. See 'Why British Women are Turning to Islam', (1993) *The Times,* 9 November, p.11; 'British Women Seek New Morality in Islam', *The Sunday Times,* 4 Sept., 1994, p.8; and 'Women Convert to Islam', *British Muslims Monthly Survey,* 2(8), 1994, p.17. See also, recent reports on Islam and women in France, 'Covered in Confusion', *The Guardian,* October 6, 1994a, pp.10-11.

3. For an in-depth discussion of the basic duties of Islam see Sarwar (1992) *Islam Beliefs and Teachings,* London: The Muslim Educational Trust, which contains within it simple and imaginative exercises to assist understanding.

4. See for example Hussain (1994) *Muslim Women,* New York: St. Martin's Press, for further discussion on Qur'anic interpretation of women's dress; and an article highlighting Muslim women's desire to seek a re-interpretation of the position of women in Muslim societies, in 'Reports on Bangladeshi Writer', *British Muslim's Monthly Survey,* 1994, 2(6), p.3.

5. 'Muslims in Britain', (1991) The Islamic Foundation and Training Unit. London: IFTU.

6. Ensuring that children remain adherents to the faith is shared by other religious groups, see for example 'Jewish identity crisis fuelled by out-of-date leaders of the faith', *The Guardian,* June 7 1994b, p.5.

7. Enabling legislation of the 1980s extended and improved parental rights with regard to their children's education incorporating changes in: choice in schooling; information on schools; pupil progress; school governance, and school discipline. Furthermore, *The European Convention on Human Rights,* to which Britain is a signatory incorporates clauses aimed at respecting parental religious and philosophical convictions with regard to their children's schooling, see A. Beddard (1980) *Human Rights and Europe,* 2nd ed., London: Sweet and Maxwell, and F. J. Jacobs (1975) *The European Convention on Human Rights,* Oxford: Clarendon Press.

8. See Union of Muslim Organisation of United Kingdom and Ireland (1976) *Guidelines and Syllabus on Islamic Education,* London: UMO.

9. Nira Yuval-Davis (1992) provides a useful discussion of this term in 'Fundamentalism, Multiculturalism and Women in Britain', in J. Donald and A. Rattansi, *Race, Culture and Difference,* London: Sage Publications, pp.278-291. See also A. Falaturi and U. Tworuschka (1991) *A Guide to the Preservation of Islam in School Textbooks,* Birmingham: Selly Oak Colleges; and F. Halliday (1994) 'The Literal versus the Liberal', *The Times Higher Educational Supplement,* 5 Aug., p.19.

Chapter 3

Islam and Education

My Lord, increase me in knowledge. (Qur'an 20:14)

Great value is placed on the acquisition and pursuit of knowledge in Islam, as well as on religious obligations. This chapter examines the relationship between Islam and education and the significance and meaning that knowledge has for Muslims[1]. The questions raised focus on: (i) the value of knowledge; (ii) types of knowledge; (iii) the role of Islamic educational institutions; and (iv) the cognitive aims of Islamic education. Further, (v) the distinction between Islamic and 'secular' philosophies of education will be considered and the potential for conflict within the educational system. Finally, these issues are explored with reference to how this impacts on everyday policy and practice in schools and the implications raised for curriculum content and methodology.

(i) The Value of Knowledge

Islam bestows great value and esteem on the pursuit of knowledge and there is ample evidence to support this, for example within the *Hadith* (sayings of the Prophet);

Seeking knowledge is a duty on every Muslim man and woman,

37

The Prophet prayed 'o my Lord do not let the sun set on any day that I did not increase my knowledge';

and especially for children:

'no gift among all the gifts of a father to his child is better than education'.

Thus, it is clear from Islamic texts that the acquisition of knowledge is valued, but which knowledge should be transmitted and in what manner?

In providing an answer to these questions it is important to start with the concept of Islam. As detailed in the previous chapter, Islam is an all-encompassing faith which provides guidance for all aspects of life and is premised on the belief that a Divine Being is responsible for the creation of the universe and all individuals are accountable for their personal conduct. Beyond this, education is seen as a process through which a child's total personality is developed in preparation for this life and the *Akhirah* or Afterlife and that 'without belief in the pivotal concept of Akhirah ... development of the feelings of responsibility and *ultimate accountability* — is unthinkable' (Sarwar, 1992, p.2). Accordingly, to a practising Muslim inspiration is drawn from God and epistemological issues, that is the theory of knowledge acquisition, are affected by this premise.

Muslims find it difficult to accept some parts of the school curriculum, not because the subjects are prohibited per se, but because their methodology of teaching is against the Guidance of Allah. The latter must be the ultimate yardstick for Muslims (ibid, p.2).

Sensitive handling of controversial issues within the curriculum and the use of withdrawal from unacceptable curricula is addressed in chapter 4, but it is instructive to note here the significance of the Islamic concept of knowledge.

The importance and value of education from an Islamic perspective is that it brings successive generations to a knowledge of their relationship with, and dependence on God. Choudhury (1993) defines 'knowledge' as comprising 'the intelligible derivation of abstract and cognitive understanding of the universe around us' (p.3). A key feature of the Islamic theory of knowledge is that all knowledge is *of* God in every sense. Thus in the Qur'anic petition, highlighted at the beginning of this chapter, 'O my Lord, increase me in knowledge', it is for knowledge of God that the Muslim prays (Hulmes, 1989). Such knowledge or 'ilm' is to be sought and acquired in ways that are consistent with the principles of Islam and seekers of knowledge of God are referred to as 'tullab' (ibid). Furthermore,

> no part of life, no thought, no way of thinking can be considered rightful if it presumes to be independent of the Islamic revelation. For Muslims, education is the means of initiating the young and immature into their *full* cultural heritage as Muslims. Education begins and ends with the revealed will of God. Muslim education is normative in quite specific ways. Education is ideologically oriented, a means to an end, not an end in itself (ibid).

There is keen interest in all aspects of knowledge which brings an individual closer to God, but also a fear of the way it may be imparted. This raises difficulties and challenges for state school educators who may inadvertently transcend the threshold of what is acceptable:

> can the western world's scientific and technological knowledge be imparted without the secularism which is so closely associated with it? It is secularism, which is eyed as a threat to Islamic cultural identity. A policy which is designed to exclude unacceptable western ideas is justified from the Muslim point of view because it is judged to be necessary for cultural survival (Hulmes, p.35).

Protecting the ummah and cultural identity, as highlighted in the previous chapter, is to be pursued through careful scrutiny of knowledge and values. Much of Western culture is considered by many Muslims to be based on materialistic, non-religious values and as such, 'the Islamic way of thinking cannot be adapted to the cultural values of the non-Islamic world' (ibid, p.37).

Incompatibility between educational philosophies are particularly apparent in aspects of the curriculum where content and values cannot be separated, and this has implications for all denominational groups;

> ... western attitudes are criticised, not only regarding Islam but regarding revealed religion in general. It may be asked if the pre-suppositions of western education place Christians, Jews and others, as

well as Muslims, at a disadvantage in schools dedicated to the pursuit of pluralist ideologies (ibid).

For Muslim children, the conflict in values as espoused by parents and the community and as reflected in the school curriculum, both formal and hidden, may cause difficulties. This tension, it is argued 'is often over-looked or disregarded, even by teachers who are genuinely trying to understand what it is like to be a Muslim in Britain today' (ibid). Accordingly:

> to understand this tension it might be better to change the more general question from 'what problems are faced by Muslims in a non-Muslim society?', to the specific question, 'What would it be like to be educated according to Islamic principles?' (ibid).

This would require a re-orientation and re-classification of knowledge. Currently within the British school system, however, it is argued that beyond literacy and numeracy,

> there is a complete culturalisation process which underlies the whole system. Every school has a cultural base, from which it derives its goals, objectives and ultimate character, and this is where the process of indoctrination ... overtly and covertly ... begins. The entire philosophy of state schools is built of *Kufr* (rejection of God and his authority) (Yusuf Islam, as cited in Raza, 1993, p.42).

Similarly, schools are seen as institutions intent on providing only a secular interpretation of reality and providing an education which 'prepares the individual for a society free from religion' (Raza, 1993, p.42). In short, there is significant value placed on knowledge within Islam and the belief that knowledge should be beneficial in helping Muslims understand both this life and the Hereafter, and the attendant obligations for adherents of the faith. The imparting of knowledge within a secularist framework devoid of religious values, however, is seen as in conflict with the overall aim of raising children within a religious context.[2]

(ii) Types of Knowledge

Essential knowledge or information which a Muslim is encouraged to seek before everything else is a correct understanding of reality and the precepts of Islam detailed in the Qur'an and other religious texts. Key points in the Qur'an characterisation of knowledge are:

(i) The concept of absolute knowledge, which is God Himself and is not fully manifest in temporal life but will be so in the Akhira or Afterlife; and

(ii) the concept of functional knowledge, an evolutionary process embracing intelligence and experience obtained in all sub-systems (Choudhury, 1993).

The primacy of Divine Law establishes the epistemological foundation of Islamisation of knowledge. Further, this provides, 'the seat where knowledge is seen to spring and convey its functional form in the intelligible, abstract and cognitive realms of reality' (ibid, p.6). Epistemological study of Qur'anic verses have, in contemporary times, been used to justify and support the Islamic perspective on knowledge: indeed, urgent debate is advocated to revitalise Islamic instruction and move beyond recital and quotation of sayings (Raza). To summarise, the Islamisation of knowledge is a process of receiving knowledge, but total knowledge will only be manifest in the Afterlife according to the Qur'an[3]. Knowledge is thus conceived within the context of religion and Qur'anic interpretation, whereas in the Western model of education, religious knowledge is constructed as a discipline in its own right, rather than a subject which permeates the curriculum and establishes the school ethos.

Ideally, secular and religious knowledge should complement each other rather than conflict but some types of knowledge may be considered unacceptable or offensive. Haneef (1979) feels a distinction can be drawn here:

knowledge inspired by Satan ... such as magic, the black arts, fortune-telling, astrology and anything related to immorality or wickedness are not permitted (ibid).

Likewise, knowledge of science and technology from non-Muslim sources are permitted but not 'the values and behaviour of people or societies which are not ruled by a strict sense of accountability to God' (ibid). Rather, the selection of knowledge should be subject to

> whatever practical and scientific knowledge they acquire to the Islamic criteria and standards, to apply whatever is appropriate and beneficial toward the building of an Islamic society governed by God's laws in all aspects of life, and to leave alone whatever is not appropriate or useful (ibid).

It would be a mistake, however to suggest that there is consensus among Muslims about the issue of selection of knowledge. Raza (1993), for example, states that Islam does not put any bar to the acquisition of knowledge but suggests: that it be planned in a balanced and interdisciplinary way; that the spiritual, moral, intellectual, imaginative, physical and emotional development of the individual are kept in view; and that the development of personality is seen in the context of man's relationship with God, and nature. Husain and Ashraf (1979) maintain that Muslim scholars do not see knowledge by itself as being harmful or dangerous but 'the extraneous values and assumptions which man imparts into it ... cause it to produce a spiritually harmful fall-out' (p.40). The selection of knowledge should accordingly be scrutinised to 're-examine the commonly accepted Western classifications of knowledge in the light of Islamic fundamentals' (ibid).

The Islamisation of knowledge is based primarily on Qur'anic concepts and the pervasiveness of Divine Law. Beginning in contemporary times with the First World Conference on Muslim Education held in Mecca in 1977, this was followed by four other world conferences focusing on Curriculum Design, Textbook Development, Teacher Education and Evaluation (Ashraf, 1994). In order to accept modern knowledge but reject the secular philosophy which is seen to accompany it, Muslims have been encouraged to establish Muslim schools and colleges. Headway has been made in this country at the Islamic Academy, Cambridge, which attracts eminent Muslim scholars from around the world. Collectively, they promote the Islamic Education movement (Ashraf, 1993), and provide academic advice to some of the private Muslim schools in Britain, highlighted in chapter 1, as well as similar institutions abroad, disseminating information on the Islamisation of knowledge.

Professor Ashraf of the Islamic Academy states that according to *Sharia* (Islamic law), all sciences, for example, are capable of being considered Islamic sciences as long as they operate within the framework of Islam and are not inconsistent with Islamic concepts and attitudes. Translating the theory into practice:

Islam embodies a general and comprehensive concept which sustains a self-contained, unique and distinctive education policy. All we have to do is base our education on this particular, unique and distinctive concept. When it comes to the means by which this can be achieved, there is no objection whatsoever to the full exploitation of every human experiment so long as it is not in conflict with the Islamic concept (Husain and Ashraf, 1979, p.44).

The Islamic Educational Trust (1991) summarises the key features of Islamic education as being:

- the acquisition of knowledge;
- imparting of knowledge;
- inculcating moral values;
- consideration of public good; and
- development of personality and emphasis on actions and responsibilities.

At face value, such an educational framework would not appear to be inconsistent with other educational philosophies except that 'inculcating moral values' would presumably rest on some religious or ideological base.

In keeping with the belief that God is the source of all knowledge that is of value to humans, religious instruction forms a vital part of a Muslim child's education. By way of illustration, the handbook on *Guidelines and Syllabus on Islamic Education* is useful here. At primary level this document suggests:

as children are too small to understand any abstract concept, the only form of religious teaching that can be imparted is by making them imitate the parents and teachers, and by conditioning their minds. They should learn by heart the Arabic version of *kalimah* [the basic creed of Islam which is, 'There is no God but Allah, and Muhammad

43

is the messenger of God'] and through the question/answer method know that they are Muslims, their religion is Islam, their prophet is Muhammad, and that Allah the Almighty and the Prophet love us and we should love and respect them and obey them (Union of Muslim Organisations, 1976, p.8).

Similarly, there is guidance for pupils at secondary school level;

This is by far the most crucial period in the mental development of children. It is a period of idealism as well as questioning, doubts, rebellion, and frustrations. In modern times, when the atmosphere of the society in the west is charged with anti-religious sentiments and attitudes, it is becoming increasingly difficult for our children to accept dogma and orthodoxy unquestioningly and to obey authority with reverence. Only by making children see religion as a historical and spiritual reality, by showing that the basis of our culture is in absolute terms, that religion alone enunciates and provides, and by presenting Islam as a natural and psychologically acceptable reality, [can] we build up within children the force that will resist evil powers and strengthen the forces of good (p.10).

The text goes on to suggest that if children choose relativism instead of absolute values, they will become spiritually, morally and intellectually confused.

Given the aims of multicultural education and the concept of pluralism, such confusion is likely to exist for Muslim children being educated in both the state system and via the Muslim home and community. Clearly, this presents challenges to teachers, especially those of religious studies, if courses not only include knowledge of a variety of world religions but also involve scrutiny of sources and the challenging of what some would see as fundamental beliefs. Further,

one consequence of this style of educational approach therefore is a deep unease about the nature of the teaching especially as it relates in the home and community. This concern is shared by many parents within Islam, Judaism and Christianity and others (Falaturi and Tworuschka, 1991, p.64).

It is for this reason that religious groups such as Muslims have developed their own forms of private supplementary education, where they have the scope to determine for themselves what constitutes knowledge and what should form curriculum content and methodology.

The appropriateness or inappropriateness of knowledge is also shared by other faiths. The Brethren, for example, a 'fundamentalist' Christian group, has actively protested to the Secretary of State for Education and Science expressing the view that information technology courses, made obligatory by the National Curriculum, conflict with their religious beliefs, and that the use of computers, television and video is strictly forbidden in the New Testament (National Curriculum Council, 1989). In the case of this group, no exemption was permitted and schools have been left to deal with the problem themselves, sometimes allowing Brethren children to sit at the back of the class and not participate, but not necessarily providing alternative arrangements or provision. Nor is the principle of the parental right of withdrawal from unacceptable curricula being addressed in this instance. Religious groups are thus left to try and correct what they feel is the damage through their own religious arrangements outside of the state education system[4]. Indeed, it has been suggested that religious groups should unite against the common enemy of secularism, for collectively they can defend the realm of the spiritual against the perceived pressures and assaults of materialism[5].

To summarise this section on types of knowledge or information valued, the overall view of Muslims is that children be exposed to such knowledge as will assist them in understanding their religion, religious obligations and identity. Whilst disagreement can exist among Muslims over what knowledge may or may not be acceptable, the overall governing factor is that knowledge should be seen firstly within the context of a religious and moral framework; and secondly, that it has a part to play in helping the individual seek religious understanding. Knowledge within an Islamic framework places emphasis on belief in a spiritual being and morality, in addition to intellectual development. Together these two premises provide for the education of the whole person within a religious context. Interestingly the *Education Reform Act* (1988)[6] conceived of education as a balance in which the spiritual as well as the religious growth of the child would be fostered. The place and quantity of religion in this instance however, is somewhat different in that a religious dimension does not permeate the school in the way advocated by religious groups. Furthermore, the potential for conflict exists within the state school system where the compulsory nature of the National Curriculum provides little room for exemption from unacceptable curriculum. Along with other religious groups, Muslims therefore, look particularly to the role played by supplementary educational institutions in supporting and maintaining religious belief and identity.

(iii) Islamic Educational Institutions

There are a variety of institutions to provide religious instruction for Muslims in Britain separate from the compulsory state education system. These normally take three forms: mosque schools or madrassahs; classes run in private homes; and private primary and secondary schools established on Islamic lines, as discussed in chapter 1.

As there are few private Muslim schools and these require parents to pay fees, the vast majority of Muslim children attend madrassahs, which were established over fifty years ago and which operate in the evenings and the weekends on a self-help community basis (Sarwar). It is calculated that about 350,000 children of compulsory school age, ie 5-16 attend, who require access to Islamic educational institutions for religious instruction (Yusuf Islam, as cited in Raza, 1993). As highlighted in the previous chapter, it is within madrassahs and private homes that this instruction takes place and cognitive aims of Islamic education are imparted. This form of supplementary education is intended to fill the perceived gap in the provision of religious and moral education within the state school system. The high number of madrassahs in Britain denote the importance parents place on passing on religious and cultural values, and are estimated at present to be over five hundred in number throughout the country (Raza, 1993).

Distinctions can be drawn between educational philosophies used in madrassahs and maintained schools which add to this discussion on the nature of knowledge and education from an Islamic perspective. In the case of madrassahs:

> the curriculum is carefully chosen. Discipline is strict, and special attention is given to memory work, particularly memorising the whole or part of the Qur'an (Hulmes, p.40).

Contrast this with education within a state school where the curriculum is typically organised in broad discrete disciplines or fields of knowledge, and teaching methodology is varied. Moreover, state schools aim to cater for children from diverse backgrounds, both religious and non-religious. In addition to the tensions inherent in this situation, statutory obligations concerning the National Curriculum have to be negotiated, making the whole concept of a common curriculum for all highly problematic.

The status of the teacher is given a special significance in Islam:

> Know, O brother, that your teacher is the begetter of your soul, just as your father is the begetter of your body. Your father gave you a physical form, but your teacher gives you a spiritual one. Your teacher nourishes your soul with learning and wisdom, and guiding it to attain everlasting bliss (Tibawi, 1972, p.35 and 39).

Teachers within Islamic societies have traditionally been perceived as models to be emulated, who mould and initiate children into a moral code; and who assume broad and expansive responsibilities which encompass the pastoral as well as the academic (Husain and Ashraf, 1979). Teachers in the madrassahs are normally drawn from the local community and have relevant cultural-religious as well as linguistic qualifications. Moreover, it is believed that if a child's teachers, as well as parents, bring the child up according to the principles of Islam, they will be rewarded in the Next-life (ibid). The perceived low status of teachers in this country is a matter of historical record and it is probably true to say that they are not generally accorded the respect or deference which prevails within the Islamic tradition[7]. Thus Muslim children operating within the two systems of education, state and madrassah, will most likely be exposed to contrasting images of teachers and teaching styles. Finally, the traditional respect that Muslims have for *ta'dib,* that is, education as conceived in Islam, 'is giving way in many cases to suspicion of Western education as they become aware that the values and beliefs implicit in the British education system (and hence imparted through both overt and hidden curriculum) are often at variance with the values and beliefs that they would wish their own children to become committed to' (Halstead, 1986, p.15).

Dissatisfaction from parents exists with the madrassah as well as the state school system. Limitations of space, inadequacy of teaching materials and methodology, and disagreement among Islamic educationalists over the appropriate way to reform and revitalise Islamic teaching for

British children in a non-Muslim society all feature as areas of concern (Raza). Other shortcomings include: 'additional financial burden on the community and academic burden on pupils; their approach and methods — including unqualified teachers, corporal punishment and rote-learning — compare unfavourably with the state system' (Halstead, p.15)[8]. In addition,

> most Muslims would tacitly agree that the old-fashioned teaching methods of the Qur'anic school are inadequate and ineffective today. At the same time, they would insist that education should be instrumental in bringing the young to a fuller understanding of Islam, and to a deeper awareness of their distinctive cultural heritage (Hulmes, p.43).

Revitalising the core of the Islam curriculum to attract and hold the interest of pupils, developing new teaching techniques and obtaining better premises are on-going concerns of Muslims (Union of Muslim Organisations, 1976; Raza, 1993; Sarwar, 1994).

Notwithstanding these criticisms of madrassahs, in the absence of state funded Muslim schools, as of writing, Muslim parents will aspire to keep their children faithful by whatever means they can. Pupils who attend Muslim schools will be exposed to Islamic education along the lines highlighted in this chapter, but the majority of Muslim children in Britain will receive such education as provided by supplementary education. Accordingly,

> madrassahs are here to stay in order to meet particular needs and give the faith communities a sense of self-fulfilment. There are grave doubts expressed by almost everyone about the nature of supplementary provision, style of teaching, methods of instruction, disciplinary procedures and many other aspects of the arrangements made at present in most madrassahs. It may be said that they meet the needs of ritualistic self-identity and are serving a purpose almost as a protest (Raza, p.44).

It is important to note, as well, that madrassahs are connected to mosques which have been established on sectarian lines, and a variety of Islamic philosophies of education are provided rather than one agreed framework.

(iv) Aims of Islamic Education

The characteristics of Islamic education centre on the acquisition of knowledge, developing moral values and nurturing an Islamic personality whereby moral and social responsibility are fostered. Definition is provided by Ashraf (1994)

> education is ... defined as the process through which the balanced growth of the total personality of a human being is achieved. According to Islam the end to be aimed at is the attainment of the status of a true representative of God on the earth (*Kalifatullah*). Education is thus not an end in itself (p.4).

In addition, education signifies the transmission of culture from one generation to another that is the cumulative experience of past generations enshrined in folklore, customs and poetry, crystallising around the basic concept of the place of man in society (Husain and Ashraf, 1979). As detailed in the earlier section on types of knowledge, experience is gathered in the form of skills passed on from generation to generation and subject to increased change; and experience is also based on constant or permanent values as embodied in religion and defined within Islamic texts. Accordingly, the aim of education from an Islamic perspective is the production of people who have a two-fold knowledge base:

> Knowledge divorced from faith is only partial knowledge, ... Islamic education consequently insists that piety and faith must be clearly recognised in syllabuses as an aim to be systematically pursued. The test of a syllabus must be whether it brings the learner nearer to an understanding of God and of the relation in which man stands to his Maker ... the test of [knowledge] validity and effectiveness will be whether it fosters or deepens awareness of the Divine Presence in the universe. If it does not it should be clearly understood to be at variance with the Islamic notion of education (ibid, p.38).

From this premise, the study of religion is regarded as the first step, but within the British state system, the importance attached to religious education is considerably less. There are clearly shared aims between the Islamic and state school system with regard to producing morally upright people, and indeed the National Curriculum includes the dimension of 'citizenship'. A single faith dimension acting as a corner-stone of education and permeating the school ethos, however, is normally absent in state schools other than within denominational institutions.

Within Islamic education ideological interpretation must be given to:

Tawhid	Unity of God
Risalat	Prophethood
Akhirah	Life Hereafter and
Khilafat	Vice Regent of Man on Earth

(Rahman, 1979)

These aspects of education are formulated by reference to Islamic texts such as the Qur'an, highlighted in the previous chapter. The significance of this religious source to this discussion is that:

> Education without religion, as independent of religion, is a contradiction in terms for a Muslim. The chief aim of Islamic education is to obtain knowledge of *God,* through the medium of the religion which God revealed in its final form to Muhammad. Anything beyond that is unnecessary. Traditionally, Muslims have resisted secular knowledge as being dangerous, although it is not knowledge itself, but the *attitude to knowledge,* which is the crucial factor (Hulmes, p.39).

It is important to highlight what may appear to be inconsistency in the arguments presented about the value of knowledge, for there is a view that the aims of Islamic education are about obtaining blind obedience, fostering ritualistic pursuit of religious duties, and showing unquestioning deference to authority. In this chapter and the previous one, children's relation to adults has been described as one in which deference is expected to be shown to authority figures such as parents and teachers. At the same time, Muslims are encouraged actively and conscientiously to seek knowledge, also highlighted in this discussion. To seek knowledge may well require pupils to question teachers, and Muslim scholars reject the notion that there is no room for this within the Islamic concept of knowledge. Raza (1993) challenges the negative suppositions about Islam and instead highlights and justifies what he feels should be considered Islamic aims of education:

- Islamic education should be investigative and critical — grounded in critical thinking and not based on blind acceptance;

- Islamic education must create a strong identity;

- Islamic education must open the door of knowledge for both sexes — they must be able to learn any skill, vocation or profession in the secular context and excel in them;

- Islamic education must be political — in the democratic system of Britain nothing can be achieved without political knowledge and an awareness of its applications;

- Islamic educational research needs to tackle the issues confronting Muslims — the gates of *Ijtihad* or independent reasoning need to be opened; and

- Islamic education should be theoretical and practical — it should bridge the gap between theory and practice (pp.46-47).

By adapting these aims, Raza argues that Islamic education can move away from a narrow concept of education to one with a positive understanding of Islam and a knowledge of the secular system.

Private Muslim schools in this country are developing educational policy along guidelines such as these, and at the same time providing flexibility in order that they incorporate the National Curriculum within an Islamic framework. As in all issues relating to Islam, implementation rests with the local community and accordingly sectarian education and its traditions are transmitted within private schools and madrassahs. There can be wide differences in interpretation and belief about what constitutes Islamic education, and guidelines proposed by scholars such as Raza have varying levels of acceptance and interpretation. A variety of Islamic philosophies of education exist within Islamic educational institutions in this country and whilst there is no consensus about methodology and content, the pivotal place of religion is the constant and agreed objective.

(v) Secularist versus Islamic Perspectives on Education

The discussion so far has outlined the valuing of knowledge; the selection of knowledge, cognitive aims of Islamic education; and the role of Islamic education institutions. What is apparent is the potential for tension and conflict between education provided in state schools and the concept and aims of Islamic education. The British National curriculum implemented as a result the *Education Reform Act* has been seen as a major challenge to Muslims and other religious groups, since,

> the curriculum used in state maintained schools is based on a secularist approach to education which claims to take a *neutral* stand on the question of religious values ...[but] a secularist approach is, however, far from being neutral. As with all faiths or world-views, secularism is based on, and promotes, a certain philosophy of life. The secularist philosophy is based on the supremacy of 'reason' and a secular religion is supposed to 'rescue' human beings from the 'shackles' of religion and religious beliefs and practices, often viewed as 'irrational'. The absolute and immutable norms and values, which for all the major religions are God-given are denied (Mabud, 1992, p.89).

Within the subject of science, for example, the concept of God is challenged and found unscientific and irrelevant:

> Values are disassociated from religion, values change along with external social change. In this scheme of things human beings are but the end product of evolution, mere earthly creatures, temporal beings possessed of mind and body but not soul or spirit (ibid).

Moreover, it is contended that all school subjects are taught from this philosophical framework and provide the prevailing ethos for the entire school (ibid). This contrasts markedly with the Islamic perspective of an unequivocal belief in God with attendant concerns over moral codes and moral responsibility detailed earlier in this chapter:

> Education in Islam is education for the total growth and development of human beings — physically, intellectually, morally and spiritually ... [and] for Muslims, education without an awareness of God is meaningless and not education at all but *indoctrination* into a particular world-view (ibid, p.89-90).

Invoking the word 'indoctrination' is particularly apposite here since that is precisely what sceptics and non-believers contend is happening within religious schools in general. This clash between religious and secular educational philosophies is highly problematic and complex. In countries such as the United States[9] and Turkey[10], for example, which claim to operate only secular curricula the issue is no less contentious, since it is arguable that no education is ever value or culture free.

A useful dichotomy between Islamic and secular models of education is provided by Halstead (1986). The principles which underline Islamic education are coherent, he says in that they are consistent with Islamic beliefs and the structure of the Muslim ummah. Explicitly, these principles are: the aim of education is to produce 'the good man'; the highest personal values are found in spiritual wisdom; the nature of morality comes from divine law; the focus of values are a community of believers; and man's attitude is that he is God's earthly vice-regent. This contrasts with the secular model of education in which, Halstead states: the aim of education is to produce a rational man/woman; highest personal values lie in the acquisition of material well-being and personal happiness; the nature of morality is relativism or subjectivism; the focus of values is individual fulfilment; and humans' attitude is to become a self-sufficient being. Where this dichotomy has direct implications for teachers is in the source of knowledge which under the Islamic model is revelation, whilst in the secular framework its basis is reason or the experimental method (ibid). The foundation of Islamic belief is traditional authority as opposed to rational autonomy; attitudes to belief are based on certainty as opposed to doubt or critical openness; the approach to religion is based on commitment and faith as opposed to scepticism; the valued state of mind is submission and reverence as opposed to ambition and pride; and finally the Islamic view of multiculturalism is moral chaos rather than the secular perspective of healthy pluralism (ibid).

Clearly, this paradigm is highly polarised and most aspects of secular education are portrayed as features most disliked by Muslims. Furthermore, writers would take issue with the view that the Islamic model of education requires blind obedience with no room for critical inquiry, as mentioned earlier. The problem is two-fold: Muslims may see state education in a predominantly negative light, as unable to satisfy the needs of religious adherents; school educators may perceive Islamic education in terms of narrow and restricted provision based on ritualistic following of religious belief.

To assist educators in the state school system about the nature and meaning of Islam,

> we need the help of Muslims who are prepared not only to interpret their own cultural pre-suppositions and defend their own beliefs, but also to show that they are aware of the real difficulties presented to the western mind by Islamic theory of knowledge (Hulmes, p.48).

This will require recognition that there may be, as Ashraf (1985) suggests, a lack of integration between Islamic and secular education, and that Islamic concepts have to be formulated in such a way as to serve as substitutes for secular concepts. It also requires state schools to examine their education policy and practice and consider the scope available to meet the educational needs of Muslim children in sensitive and sensible ways.

Whilst Britain is in reality a multicultural and multifaith society, critics argue that a secular monocultural perspective predominates within the schools, aimed at achieving social harmony and marginalising all religions:

> ... to try to promote multiculturalism after disassociating all faiths from those cultures will not be accepted by Muslims ... Muslims do not expect the curriculum in state schools to be Islamic. What they do expect, however, is that the multicultural, multifaith character of Britain will be reflected in the curriculum and in the school ethos (Mabud, 1992 p.91).

The issue of multicultural education is discussed in greater depth later in this book. Note here, however, the Muslim perception of secularist/multicultural education as being inimical to their well-being. The predominance of the secularisation of society into a more socially cohesive form threatens to undermine Muslim identity;

> the authorities forget that their secularist policy is regarded by the Muslim community as an attempt to brainwash Muslim children, uproot them from their cultural moorings, create tension between home and school, parents and children, and what is most dangerous for the upcoming generation, it does not provide children with cer-

tainty and a reliable, sustaining and accepted and acceptable norm to fall back upon (Ashraf, as cited in Mabud, pp.91-92).

Secondly, in discussing the educational needs of Muslim children; it is important 'to avoid interpreting the problems of Muslim parents and pupils solely in western secular terms' (Mabud, p.96). Ignoring the relevance and significance of religion within the lives of Muslim children, is to miss totally the interconnectedness between faith and education; between content and acquisition of knowledge; and between education and moral responsibility in this life and the next. This is reflected in multicultural teaching which is claimed to be counter-productive to the Muslim interest:

> the formal education received in British schools is both inadequate and superfluous so far as Islam is concerned. The external descriptive approach to the ritual and liturgy of Islam belongs to an un-Islamic phenomenology. For Muslims, such an approach is inescapably reductionist and inadequate (Hulmes, 1989, p.31).

Moreover, the education imbibed in state schools is akin to questioning and challenging the notion of the existence of God, whereas that within madrassahs is of a different nature:

> even at the best of times 'faith' is presented as a narrow, spiritualistic and rather confusing concept. 'Religions' are grouped together and offered as a hotch-potch optional subject. Therefore the whole identity of the Muslim character and system of intellectual enquiry is minimalised from the very beginning (ibid).

Likewise, some Muslims are suspicious of the inclusion of Islam within a multifaith curriculum and the inability of schools to adequately convey the religion's features and dimensions. Furthermore, 'Muslims are suspicious of what passes for cultural pluralism in the West as potentially inimical to the ummah [community]' (Hulmes, p.34). What comes across most strikingly from these comments is both the fear Muslim communities have that their religion and identity is undermined by British society, and the lack of knowledge and success which schools are perceived to have in interpreting Islam in a satisfactory manner. The following two chapters examine further the role that educationalists play in reducing some of the anxieties expressed by Muslim communities. Broader philosophical and

55

pedagogical issues raised by this discussion are explored further in chapters 6 and 7.

Conclusion

Islam places great value and significance on the acquisition of knowledge and sees it as part of an individual's development and journey in discovering God. Set within a religious context, the aim of education from an Islamic perspective is to pursue and acquire knowledge and at the same time to inculcate and transmit values concerning morality, responsibility and accountability. Knowledge is not divorced from religion, rather the two complement each other as part of a wide-ranging educational experience. A variety of approaches have been presented by Muslim writers concerning what should be the aims of Islamic education in the context of life within a secular society, but the pivotal importance of religion and religious values is characteristic of all Islamic philosophies of education. Conflict is perceived between Western-secular and Islamic philosophies of education in which different emphasis and interpretation is placed on concepts such as critical inquiry. Furthermore, it is suggested that Western modes of thinking and conceptualisation are inadequate to explain Islamic concepts of educational issues. Finally, multicultural education is seen at best as an inadequate, ill-informed attempt to explain tokenistically different religions operating within a pluralistic society; and at worst as an imposed ideology with a dominant slant on non-religion aimed at undermining belief in religion. Notwithstanding these very real concerns, the majority of Muslim children are taught within the state school system and understanding and responding to their needs is an on-going process. This forms the basis of the following chapter, in which accommodation of needs is addressed with reference to current educational practice.

Notes

1. I would like to acknowledge the kind assistance of Asaf Hussain and Qamar Chaudhri in reading over this chapter to ensure accuracy in interpretation.
2. For trends towards secularisation, see B. Jowell et al (1989) *British Social Attitudes*, Aldershot: Gower.
3. For more on this theme see I. R. al-Faruqi (1982) *Islamisation of Knowledge: General Principles and Workplan*, Hendon: International Institute of Islamic Thought; J. S. Idris (1987) 'The Islamisation of the Sciences: Its Philosophy and Methodology', *The American Journal of Islamic Social Sciences*, 4(2) pp.201-208; and I. Ba-Janus (1988) 'Future Directions in Islamisation of Knowledge', *The American Journal of Islamic Social Sciences*, 5(1) pp.13-28.
4. For more on supplementing education see M. McLean (1985) 'Private Supplementary Schools and the Ethnic Challenge to State Education in Britain', in C. Brock and W. Tulasiewicz (eds) *Cultural Identity and Educational Policy*, London: Croom Helm; and 'Why Discipline is the Key to Good Education', *The Voice*, Sept. 20, 1994, p.12 in which it is stated that 'Black Saturday schools' in Britain, for example, compensate for the inadequacies of the mainstream education system.
5. See 'Religions Unite Against Secularism', *British Muslims Monthly Survey*, 1994, 2(2), p.13.
6. *Education Reform Act* 1988, London: HMSO, ch.40.
7. See for example A. Tropp (1957) *The School Teachers*, London: Heinemann; D. Wardle (1976) *English Popular Education 1760-1902*, London: Cambridge Press; and H. Hodge (1899) 'The Problem Teacher', *Fortnightly Review*, 65, pp.853-862.
8. For more on the teachings of Islam in Qur'anic schools see for example J. S. Nielsen (1981) 'Muslim Education at Home and Abroad', *British Journal of Religious Education*, Vol. , pp.94-99 and p.107, and Association of Muslim Schools (1990) *Islamic Studies Guide*, Transvaal, South African Institute for Islamic Educational Research.
9. See J. O. Voll (1991) 'Islamic Issues for Muslims in the United States', in Y. Y. Haddad, *Muslims in America*, Oxford: Oxford University Press.
10. See *Turkish Daily News*, April 20, 1994, p.B3 'Religious 'Bias' in the West Against Islam', p.B3.

Notes

Chapter 4

Pupil needs

Good multicultural education should be sensitive to special needs (Jeffcoate, 1981, p.32).

Muslim pupils have special needs by virtue of their religious identity and adherence, as described in the previous two chapters. This account draws predominantly on the work of Islamic writers, who identify three main categories of needs: (i) religious/cultural; (ii) curricular; and (iii) general. The analysis should be seen within the context of the principles of Islam outlined earlier, and the implications of what it means to be a Muslim with specific duties and obligations which fall to parents and children. Finally, this chapter makes reference to the relevant National Curriculum documents and contains suggestions and initiatives within each section for translating the theory into practice, and exploring the scope for accommodation of needs in schools.

(i) Religious/Cultural Needs

Daily Prayers

The opportunity to practice the faith in accordance with Islamic principles is an important aspect of everyday life. For Muslims, a major aspect of their faith is the duty to pray five times a day, an obligation which does not cease on schooldays! The five prayer times are:

59

Fayr	— between dawn and sunrise;
Zuhr	— between midday and mid afternoon;
'Asr	— between middle noon and sunset;
Maghib	— just after sunset; and
Isha	— between nightfall and daybreak.

(Sarwar, 1994, p.18).

The timing of prayer sessions vary according to seasonal variations but 'Zuhr' and possibly 'Asr' fall within the school day.

By about the age of ten, Muslim children are expected to take prayer duties seriously but they face the dilemma of being unable to fulfil obligations within the confines of the classroom. Schools can respond by either creating flexibility in the timetable at midday or by permitting children to withdraw for a short time to observe their religious duty. Schools could provide a prayer room for the activity, which is normally of a few minutes duration, and also washing facilities adjacent to the prayer room, for Muslims have a particular concept of hygiene which demands *wudu* or ablution before worship. This requires only running water or containers of water (McDermott and Ashan, 1980). Friday prayers or *Salatul Jamu'ah*, have special significance and should be said in a congregation, preferably a mosque (Sarwar). An extended lunch or early finishing time could be considered, or suitably qualified Imams can be invited into school to lead prayers. Some schools in Bradford and Tower Hamlets have implemented change along these lines, demonstrating that state education can be responsive to the religious needs of pupils. An interesting case was recently reported of a Staffordshire school which converted its photographic dark-room into a prayer room so that the sole Muslim pupil could have a place set aside for daily prayers[1].

School Assemblies

Collective acts of worship have always been a part of the school day in Britain and section 25 of the *Education Act* (1944)[2] reaffirms this aspect, subject to withdrawal on conscientious grounds. This principle has latterly been incorporated into the *Education Reform Act* (1988)[3]: '... all pupils in attendance at a maintained school shall on each school day take part in an act of collective worship.' (DES, 1989a, section 6). The new legislation adds that the act of worship 'shall be wholly or mainly of a broadly Christian character' (section 7).

Where there is a sizeable proportion of pupils from other faiths, schools may request permission to hold alternative acts of worship by applying to the locals standing advisory council for religious education (SACRE). Religious instruction is likewise countenanced in terms of Christianity:

> any agreed syllabus shall reflect the fact that the religious traditions in Great Britain are in the main Christian (section 8(3)).

Interestingly, this clause goes on to say 'whilst taking into account the principles and practices of the other principal religions represented in Great Britain'. These religious clauses have direct impact on Muslims and pupils of other faiths. Notwithstanding the tide of secularisation[4], state schools in Britain are perceived as Christian schools. Some Muslim parents feel that Christian-orientated worship is unacceptable and are encouraged to invoke their right to absent their children (Muslim Educational Trust (MET), 1992; Iqra Trust, 1991a). This occurred in Eccles where 33 children were withdrawn from an Anglican school because their request for instruction in Islam was denied (TES, 1990). Much criticism of the new legislation has arisen, since the notion of a predominantly Christian assembly totally ignores the reality of multicultural and multi-faith Britain.

The right to withdraw children from religious assemblies was enshrined in the *Education Act* (1944), and the *Education Reform Act* (1988); and is upheld in the more recent *Education Act* (1993)[5]. Parents' rights to have their religious convictions respected is also enshrined in the *European Convention on Human Rights,* to which Britain is a signatory[6]. Moreover, the Government's 'Circular on Religious Education and Collective Worship' (1994)[7] emphasises that 'the parental right to withdraw a child from attending collective worship should be freely exercisable' and there is no obligation to give reasons for the request (section 85). Withdrawal normally takes the form of a written request to the headteacher and is available to children of all religious persuasions. The practical implications of this in compliance is that the school continues to assume responsibility for supervision. In some schools, instruction in an alternative act of worship is offered. Costs incurred may fall to parents or the local community for withdrawal from the collective act of worship if pupils constitute a minority faith group (section 88). As stated earlier, in cases where the religious group is in the majority, the law permits the headteacher to apply for a determination that Christian worship is inappropriate, and the 'statutory worship' changes its character. There may be occasions within schools where there are a variety of religious groups represented and, accordingly, a number of 'determinants' may be sought and acts of worship arranged for each group (sections 68-76). Finally, the 1993 Education Act requires each local education authority to regularly review the Agreed Syllabus for Religious Education (section 29). The School Curriculum and Assessment Authority (SCAA) is presently producing Religious Education syllabuses which may be used as a basis for locally agreed syllabuses[8].

From the point of view of teaching:

> Muslims have no difficulties studying other religious beliefs and practices, ... what causes difficulty is the implication that the study of Christianity is more important and more relevant than the study of Islam ... Whilst appreciating the need to understand and respect other faiths, it is wrong for a curriculum to suggest that other religions are subordinate to Christianity. Indeed, it would be very damaging for children to grow up believing that to be really British and contribute meaningfully to society, a Christian background is almost essential (Sarwar, 1994, pp.7-8).

Muslims and other religious groups may well interpret the new legislation as implying that Christianity is superior to, rather than equal to other faiths. The spirit if not the letter of the law appears to be conveying this message.

The presence of a variety of faith groups within one school complicates the issue of providing collective worship which is both relevant and applicable for all pupils. Notwithstanding the legal and moral complexities, some schools have continued to present collective acts of worship which are multi-faith, guided by representatives from resource centres and local authority advisers. The Bradford Inter-Faith Centre is one such body responding to schools grappling with issues contained within religious education (Lodge, 1990). Furthermore, invitations to Imams and Islamic scholars to visit and give talks for all children is recommended (McDermott and Ashan, 1980), as well as the provision of

Islam being taught in schools (Anwar, 1982). (This latter point is elaborated within the section on curricular needs.)

Religious Celebrations

Important festivals such as 'Id-al Fitr' and 'Id-al Adha' (von Grunebaum, 1976) are observed. The former celebrates the end of the fasting month of Ramadan, and the latter recognises the accomplishment of the rite of Hajj or pilgrimage to Mecca (Iqra Trust, 1991a). At both celebrations, Muslims are obliged to attend the mosque early in the morning for the Id prayers, and afterwards the day is normally spent celebrating with friends and relatives. Absence from school is often required and exercising discretion in this instance is in keeping with the tradition in Britain of permitting days of absence for religious celebration, pursuant to section 39 of the 1944 Education Act. This provision has been taken up by pupils of other minority faiths in Britain such as those of the Ukrainian Catholic church. Schools with a high proportion of Muslim pupils could possibly arrange to take their occasional closure days at these times of Islamic celebration (Iqra Trust, 1991a).

School Diet and Fasting

A further aspect of the Muslim faith concerns diet and fasting. The Qur'an provides guidance on diet and its importance for good health. In many matters of life, Muslims describe things as being *halal* which means permissible, or *haram* which means forbidden. This distinction is used with regard to food matters. Pork is forbidden in all forms including products containing its derivatives (Sarwar, 1994). All other meat is permitted; as long as it has been slaughtered by a Muslim following Islamic principles which ensures it is then halal (ibid). The provision of halal meat in the school catering facilities is therefore required (Iqra Trust, 1991a, Karim, 1976). Some local education authorities do provide halal food in the school canteen[9] or offer vegetarian food which does not have 'any animal by-products or alcoholic substances' used in the cooking or preparation (Sarwar, p.20). As with the needs of other faiths such as Judaism[10], distinction over permissible and forbidden food also extends to the use of separate utensils when serving halal/vegetarian or non-halal food. (Further details on halal products and suppliers are provided in the appendix.)

Fasting occurs during the month of Ramadan, normally in the spring term, and secondary pupils in particular are encouraged to practice this aspect of the faith. The provision of rooms other than the dining area is a concession required for those pupils abstaining during religious occasions (Iqra Trust, 1991a). Discretion is also possible in physical education lessons during the month of Ramadan so that less strenuous activities are pursued (Carroll and Hollinshead, 1993). Avoidance of swimming would also be welcomed since under Islamic requirements no water should enter the mouth during fast times, except for *wudu* (Sarwar). The National Curriculum guidance on Physical Education (1992) provides for 'differentiation' in teaching (section 18)[11]. This could be broadly interpreted to accommodate Muslim pupils by planning a programme of study with appropriate tasks at particular times of the year to incorporate religious considerations.

School Dress

School dress is an everyday practical need which has specific significance to Muslim children. Muslims are expected to practice a high level of decency in all activities (McDermott and Ashan, 1980). Requirements outlined in the Qur'an and the Sunnah prayers provide an Islamic dress code which holds that 'modesty is the uppermost concern' (Sarwar, p.17). This becomes particularly important for girls after the age of puberty, and some Muslims believe that 'the whole body — except the hands and the face — should be covered' (ibid). In order to ensure that the hair is not visible, a *hijab* or covering is required and a headscarf is often worn.

There is no consensus among Muslims about the correct attire and schools might understandably be confused about the different degrees of covering up by children described by the generic term of 'Muslim'. Dress sense is often based on a family's personal interpretation of what is appropriate for Muslims and a variety of dress forms are worn by Muslim women in Britain ranging from: a *burqa* or cloak-like garment with veil; the *hubaya* or long gown; the *shalwar kameez* — loosely fitting trousers under a long-sleeved tunic; and the more common *hijab* or headscarf. In keeping with Islamic principles of modesty, many Muslims believe that girls need to cover themselves in, for example, *shalwar kameez* and in some instances the *hijab* (Karim, 1976; Mabud, 1992). Secondary school girls may need to wear 'shalwar' or trousers instead of skirts.

64

For some Muslims, the tradition of females covering their heads may be cultural rather than religious in origin and determined by the social-economic status afforded by dress style. Werbner (1981) notes the significance of dress among Muslim women and the connection between the traditional burqa and social class. There is a variety of attitudes amongst Muslims themselves towards the requirement for females to cover their heads and some associate the burqa with economic status and educational attainment, rather than simply with religious identity. Palmer (1990) asks whether some of the indignation expressed by Muslim parents about their daughters' dress and conduct at school relates to the meaning these things have in the social and cultural spectrum of their own cultures.

Where Muslim families and communities feel it appropriate to cover the head, the girls might well wish to do so, both within and beyond the school gates. This has led to objections from some schools, on the grounds of health and safety (Spencer, 1990). If a pupil is denied admission to school unless she modifies her dress code, this may be interpreted as a requirement which compromises her religious convictions. Sarwar (1994) maintains that there is no reason why a suitably-tied hijab cannot be both safe and acceptable, and many schools have consulted with local communities and made arrangements regarding the wearing of scarves to the satisfaction of all parties concerned.

The wearing of the hijab by Muslim girls in secular state schools has prompted heated debate in Europe, and also at tertiary level in Turkey which, although a Muslim country, has a secular government and education system[12]. A political storm has developed in France, in which politicians, educationalists and Muslim communities have all become involved in what is perceived to be the difficulty the French are experiencing in coming to terms with a sizeable and increasing Muslim population (Follain, 1989). In Britain, disagreement over the wearing of hijab has only arisen in isolated instances and since the 1970s many schools have devised policy which allows the adaptation of school dress in school in accordance with personal and religious convictions. Indeed, for many teachers school dress may appear to be an issue of little consequence since the matter was effectively resolved several years ago. There are, however, schools around the country which are still in the process of negotiating the acceptability of school dress[13].

The requirement that school dress demonstrates modesty and decency with respect for Islamic principles includes boys also. Both sexes have an obligation to ensure their clothes are loose fitting and not transparent (Sarwar). An issue recently receiving attention concerns the wearing of beards. Incidents have been reported of Muslim boys being sent home from school and denied re-admission unless clean-shaven[14]. Schools have permitted Sikh boys to wear beards, partly to avoid litigation as occurred in the case of *Mandla v. Dowell Lee* (1983)[15]. In this instance the court held that Sikhism constitutes an ethnic group and refusal to admit a pupil wearing a turban contravened the *Race Relations Act* (1976)[16]. As a result, certain practices of Sikhism have been accommodated by schools, including the wearing of a beard. Sarwar maintains that, since

> to keep a beard is the most natural way to follow the Sunnah, schools should not discourage pupils who choose to practice their faith in this way (p.18).

Muslims cannot invoke the same legislation as Sikhs as they cannot claim racial but only religious discrimination, but some Muslims are calling for the right to wear a beard to be extended to them. Similarly, boys from other groups have expressed a desire to adopt a hairstyle consistent with religious identity. For example, Rastafarian pupils are challenging school rules on dress which prohibit their retaining their 'dreadlocks', which they argue is of religious significance and part of cultural heritage (The *Voice*, 1994a). Legal authority for this lies in the *Children Act* (1989), which stipulates that teachers should take into account a child's religious and cultural background[17]. Schools are therefore being required to review policy on school dress and hairstyle so that it affords equal rights regardless of race, religion or gender.

Standards of modesty for both male and female Muslims have direct implications for physical education and attire. A compulsory part of the National Curriculum at every key stage, physical education covers swimming, gymnastics, games, dance, athletics, outdoor and adventurous activities[18]. Physical exercise is not inconsistent with Islam, explains Sarwar, but there are 'basic Islamic requirements which must be satisfied, such as prohibition on indecent clothing and free-mixing between the sexes' (p.12). This means in practical terms that Muslim children should be permitted to wear sportswear compatible with the Islamic dress code, and the use of tracksuits and leotards normally satisfies this requirement. Communal changing and shower facilities are not acceptable. The issue of physical education and ethnicity has been recently examined and one group of researchers concluded:

> it is not the shower itself which causes the problem, but communal showers, where pupils have to undress and shower with other children (Carroll and Hollinshead, 1993, p.66).

Certainly, Muslim children are required to cover themselves up to preserve their modesty (Sarwar). One possibility is to allow pupils to delay showering until they reach home: 'an increasing number of schools permit this, and have found that it poses no hazard to health' (ibid, p.12). This would avoid 'the potential for the psychological effect of enforced communal nudity' (ibid). The potential for harm to all children, regardless of religious or philosophical background is noted by consultant child psychiatrist Wilkins (1986), who maintains:

> compulsory group nakedness constitutes a gross infringement upon the civil liberties of a child and is a prospect no adult would willingly contemplate ... [it] is the quintessential humiliation for the pubescent child (as cited in Sarwar, 1994, p.13).

Some schools are attempting to re-schedule physical education to the final period of the day or to allow showering in the privacy of the home. Interestingly, it is noted that 'such moves have, according to some teachers, provoked a noticeable increase in the interest shown by children in sport' (ibid). School policy based on flexibility in the timing and requirement of showers, as well as single sex groups and a school dress code compatible with Islamic principles all serve the needs of Muslim children and ensure their comfort in participating in educational activities. Collectively these issues form aspects of religious/cultural needs affecting everyday life in school.

(ii) Curriculum Needs

The curriculum can be used to address issues in general such as language and customs or specific problems such as prejudice and racism. There are also aspects of the curriculum which can cause special concern for Muslim parents and their children, and withdrawal from class because of unacceptable or offensive curricula is a possibility to accommodate Muslim sensitivities. This may not be educationally desirable since such a move flies in the face of efforts to foster multiculturalism but it may not be possible to satisfy the religious convictions of all parents. Accordingly, efforts have been made by theorists to identify areas of concern within the curriculum and to suggest ways in which schools can respond sensitively and sensibly to help ensure Muslim children have access to all lessons.

Sex Education

It is not uncommon for parents of both religious and non-religious backgrounds to question the content and delivery of sex education lessons. The *Education (No.2) Act* (1986) gave governors the option of deciding whether sex education should be offered in schools or not[19]. Added to this, the *Education Reform Act* sets the National Curriculum within a framework of a balanced and broadly based curriculum which 'promotes the spiritual, moral, cultural, mental and physical development of pupils... and prepares such pupils for the opportunities, responsibilities and experiences of adult life' (sec. 2(a)(b)). Sex education is clearly an important part of this broad educational aim of preparing children for responsible and informed adulthood. Legislation has also recognised the importance of parents as key figures in their children's upbringing and that sex education teaching offered by schools should be complementary to and supportive of the role of parents.

More recently, the *Education Act* (1993) removes the governors' option clause and sex education is now compulsory for all children at secondary level. Primary schools governors are required to consider whether sex education should form part of the secular curriculum so here it remains optional (section 241)[20]. Also included within the subject of sex education is Acquired Immune Deficiency Syndrome (AIDS), Human Immunedeficiency Virus (HIV) and any other sexually transmitted disease (section 241(2)). National Curriculum Science is the only place in which sex education is mandatory in the curriculum. Accordingly, only 'biological facts' should be incorporated within sex education as a compulsory section, subject to review in 1995: the other issues remain outside the National Curriculum and therefore provide the possibility of withdrawal from what might be considered unacceptable or offensive curricula (section 241(2)). Exercising this right when appropriate is noted by McDermott and Ashan (1980), Anwar (1982) and Mabud (1992).

As outlined in the previous two chapters, the Islamic view on life is that all actions should be directed to the attainment of God's pleasure which is rewarded in this life and the Hereafter. Qur'anic principles dictate that the pursuit of knowledge is an obligation on all Muslim men and women in preparation of becoming a worthy servant of Allah. Added to this are requirements pertaining to piety, modesty and decency. It is within a framework based on these principles that sex education should be set.

In *Sex Education: The Muslim Perspective*, Sarwar (1989) states that 'the need for ... sex education is not in doubt. The debate is concerned with, where, how and by whom this education should be given' (p.6). He adds,

> it is probably fair to say that the majority of Muslim parents would be happy if there was no sex education at all in schools. Since this is not possible, they would like to be informed beforehand about the contents of such education ... [and] look for ways by which to safeguard their children from the undesirable effects of liberal sex education (p.7).

Sarwar recommends that information about human physical development should be presented objectively to children, with parental consent after the age of ten, i.e. final year of primary or first year of secondary school, as part of health and hygiene or personal and social education lessons. The Qur'an contains specific information pertaining to many of the issues inherent in such lessons, such as menstruation, childbirth and marriage (2.22), and attention is given to matters of personal health and hygiene.

The key principle for discussion of sex education is that for Muslims sexuality is envisaged within lawful marriage. As marriage is the only basis of family life countenanced, extra-marital sex is wholly unacceptable. The sexual etiquettes of Islam, notes Sarwar, stress modesty and a sense of morality and excludes extra-marital sex and homosexuality. A difficulty arises, therefore, when sex education is seen to move from factual knowledge on human development to sexual activity outside Islamic boundaries. Accordingly, argues Sarwar,

> Muslim parents feel strongly that their children should be exempted from those parts of sex education which deal with extra-marital

relationships especially when explicit material on human sexuality is used (p.7).

Specific issues arising in sex education classes may cause potential problems. For example, as Islam does not contemplate sexual activity outside of marriage, the issue of contraception is not considered a major area of concern. Where it is used it is within marriage on grounds of the mother's or child's health (Sarwar, p.11). Similarly, abortion is only permitted when continuation with the pregnancy might 'endanger the mother's life' (ibid, p.12). Islamic views on marriage, childbirth, contraception and abortion show clearly the potential for conflict, and consultation is required to ensure and reassure that the delivery of this aspect of the sex education curriculum does not offend Islamic convictions.

Schools need to be clear themselves about what arrangements are made under sex education policy for parents to avail themselves of the right to withdraw their children from this part of the curriculum. Again, Sarwar is instructive here:

> Muslims are not against sex education per se. Islam encourages all purposeful human actions, and this includes sex education as part of a broad and balanced curriculum... What Islam not only discourages but also prohibits is the promotion of obscenity, irresponsibility and shameful acts which debase human beings (p.9).

Clearly, headteachers and school governors need to be aware of the strong views Muslims (and non-Muslims) may hold on sex education and provide consultation that allows opportunity for review of the curriculum and resources to be employed. Education policy which recognises and responds to the issues concerning content and methodology will help to diminish the potential for anxiety among parents. Sex education taught within the context of family life and morality, as countenanced in the *Education No.2 Act* (1986) is unlikely to cause offence. To avoid creating the need for parents to withdraw their pupils from such lessons, regular and up-to-date consultation will be required, especially since this part of the curriculum is rapidly expanding. Teaching about AIDS, HIV and other sexually transmitted diseases means that schools will need to ensure that parents are well briefed on how and where these issues appear in the curriculum, so as to allay fears and prevent withdrawal. One possibility is that sex education is taught in single sex groupings.

70

Presently, there is ongoing debate about the provision of sex education and its appropriateness, or otherwise, to the maturity and chronological age of the children[21]. On this matter, Sarwar (1989) states that Muslims believe that children should only be given such education when they and their parents feel they are ready to receive it. This should be possible to accommodate, since the 1993 Act stipulates that school governors should have regard to representations from the community with due regard to cultural or religious factors influencing the discussion of sexual issues[22]. The controversial nature of this part of the curriculum leaves educators walking a tight-rope, however, between providing overly-explicit material, or leaving pupils ignorant and ill-informed[23].

Whilst withdrawal from unacceptable or offensive curricula is clearly permissible, it is not just about children being absent from one aspect of the school curriculum. It is about the potential for breakdown of the home-school link and should be seen as a last resort and not an automatic reaction, with a view to keeping the door open for negotiation and re-negotiation. This will help to reassure parents of the recognition of a need for 'the protection of the Islamic consciousness of Muslim children in the state system' (ibid, p.33). For some Muslim parents, only a Muslim school can ensure the protection of this Islamic consciousness. Since the majority of Muslim children are educated within the state system, a pathway and balance has to be found that incorporates the demands of legislation and the respects of parents

Language Instruction

Choice of language instruction has come under review. Under British law, the Education Reform Act (1988) stipulates that a modern language must form part of the compulsory foundation subjects for all 11-16 year olds. The National Curriculum requires all children aged 11-16, Key stages 3 and 4, to study a foreign language as one of their foundation subjects. This is optional at primary school level. While French, German or Spanish have traditionally been taught as second languages, schools are being encouraged to provide language options in Urdu, Gujerati or Arabic. It has been argued that for Muslims, Mecca is the centre of the world, not Brussels (McCrystal, 1990). Before the National Curriculum was implemented, Urdu for example was offered for the General Certificate in Secondary

Education and such initiatives should be promoted (Mabud, 1992). This is in keeping with the Bullock Report (1975) which stated that:

> no child should be expected to cast off the language and culture of the home as he crosses the school threshold (p.286).

A choice of European languages is offered in most schools but:

> in schools with Muslim pupils it would be educationally sound to offer Arabic and the community languages among the modern language options. Such an option for Muslim children would combine greater access to their religious and cultural heritage with the benefits of wider linguistic skills and an enhanced sense of self-esteem and achievement (Sarwar, p.26).

Headteachers could solicit responses from parents regarding *community languages,* such as Bengali, Turkish or Urdu, to ascertain demand and consider making such provision a reality. Again, resources and particularly finance are key factors. However, there are legal as well as moral obligations for the education system to be proactive in this matter. Provision for mother tongue education is contained in a directive passed by the European Economic Community in 1977 which places a commitment on Britain to effect suitable measures (Liell and Sanders, 1984). At a time of anticipated cut-backs in funding for staff working with children whose first language is not English, the issue of mother tongue teaching is of particular concern[24], and will be discussed further in chapter 6.

Islamic Dimensions

Changing the formal curriculum to reflect an Islamic dimension is promoted (Anwar, 1982; Hulmes, 1989; Muslim Educational Trust, 1992) and encouraged as a way to raise esteem and cultural identity (Sarwar, 1983). Set within the National Curriculum Guidelines, there is potential scope for inclusion of non-Western perspectives within the options of subjects such as history and geography. Indeed the history syllabus could be used to reflect the Muslim contribution to Science and civilisation in order to challenge negative perceptions of Islam and Muslims (MET). Attempts have been made to design a balanced curriculum in which minority groups are depicted in an accurate way and Black and ethnic minority achievements are acknowledged and included within the curriculum (*The Voice*, 1994b). The National Curriculum recommends schools to take account of ethnic and cultural diversity, and there is potential scope for the inclusion of non-Western perspectives and the avoidance of ethnocentric bias. (This theme of cultural diversity in the curriculum is developed further in chapters 5 and 6).

Other initiatives involve Religious Education programmes encouraging children to study Islam at GCSE level, either as a subject in its own right or as part of a GCSE in Religious Studies. The Muslim Educational Trust, together with the University of London Examinations and Assessment Council, has developed a syllabus along these lines to be available from 1994 with a first examination in 1996[25]. Providing the opportunity to study Islam in a GCSE programme is a practical option which could be open to all pupils.

Finally an appropriate Islamic dimension can be provided if schools stock authoritative books for relevant information on Islam and British Muslims. The authenticity and factual accuracy of such books needs to be checked and schools are encouraged to consult with 'reputable' Islamic/Muslim organisations in Britain. Clearly, confusion exists here for heads of departments and librarians over what constitutes reliable publications. The Muslim Educational Trust provides guidance and the appendix to this book lists a range of potential sources.

Dance, Music and Art

Consensus is lacking among Muslims over the suitability of dance, music and art in the curriculum or whether they constitute un-Islamic activities. Art, music and physical education, which includes dance, were designed to complete the legal framework of National Curriculum Foundation subjects. Collectively they were conceived as assisting in the 'cultural and physical development' of the child as part of a broad and balanced curriculum[26]. The Muslim Educational Trust (MET) states:

> dance has no academic significance or value, nor does it contribute positively to meaningful human knowledge. Islam, as an all-embracing way of life, has specific limits on certain topics: these include a modest dress code, the prohibition of many types of music ... and the prohibition of free mixing of the sexes (Sarwar, 1994, p.13).

Accordingly,

since most, if not all forms of dance involve either some or all of the above and manage to contravene all of them at one time or another, it is clear to see that dance as is generally practised is not allowed for Muslims (p.14).

Conversely,

some Muslims may accept folk and cultural dances taught to single sex groups (Iqra Trust, 1991a, p.14).

The latter view provides some leeway for schools anxious to make arrangements which do not contravene Islamic sensibilities and some schools have experimented with varieties of dance expression. Indeed, dance is interpreted within physical education guidance notes as being placed in a broad cultural context with three interrelated categories: popular culture; traditional or folk dance from different countries; and historical dances of the past[27]. Finally on the issue of dance, a case was recently reported in which a 13 year old Muslim boy refused to join a co-educational aerobic dance class because of his Islamic principles[28]. Parental permission for withdrawal from the lesson was denied and after consultations the matter was resolved by the pupil working behind a 'modesty screen'. Whilst a successful resolution was thus effected, it is noteworthy that none of the other Muslim parents in the school, which has 70 per cent Muslim children on roll, objected to the dance curriculum. This confirms the case made throughout this book that there is no consensus among Muslim parents, as with any other religious grouping, on a number of issues within the curriculum, dance being a case in point.

Likewise, *music* has the potential for causing problems. Music is a foundation subject in the National Curriculum at the first three Key stages and is optional at Key stage four[29]. A range of music is included, and performing, listening and responding to a variety of music. Islamic guidelines on the role of music in the curriculum revolves firstly around whether it contributes positively to knowledge acquisition and secondly, whether it enables the pupil to be aware of God and their role in life. Sarwar believes these principles have not been given consideration in the formulation of music within the curriculum. This point is discussed further:

every culture and ethnic group has its own traditions of folk music. However in Islam, the only 'music' which transcends culture and ethnicity and is universally accepted by all Muslims is the recitation of the Holy Qur'an (Iqra Trust, 1991a, p.13).

Again, there is no consensus among Muslim parents on the issue, thus leaving educationalists in a dilemma:

> schools with Muslim parents may find that their parents offer apparently conflicting advice, thoughts and beliefs on the subject of music. Some parents will think that it is perfectly in order for their children to study music in school: some will be happy with certain aspects of the subject but unhappy with others; some will be completely unhappy that their children are forcibly exposed to a *haram* (forbidden) activity. The matter largely depends on the degree of practice of the faith within the home and the amount of interest that the parent takes in what their children are studying at school (Sarwar, 1994, p.15).

In analysing whether music in the curriculum is haram (forbidden) or *halal* (permissible), Sarwar states that according to the majority of Islamic scholars the use of musical instruments is not allowed; this includes the instruments and also singing musical accompaniment. Muslim children would appear to be restricted with regard to playing musical instruments. However, there is some scope for inclusion, one suggestion being that we:

> allow Muslim children to study musical theory in relation to the human voice and perform unaccompanied songs of an Islamic nature [in praise of God and the Creation etc.] (ibid, p.16).

Similarly, younger pupils may be permitted to participate in lessons where music is being used to sensitise children to the natural world of sounds (Iqra Trust). If National Curriculum guidelines can be interpreted in such a way that scope is provided to do this and religious beliefs are thus respected, then withdrawal from music lessons need not be necessary. Accommodations and variations of this nature are particularly important to consider in schools where Muslim children form the majority, otherwise the withdrawal of the vast majority of the class makes teaching music extremely difficult and potentially liable to cancellation! Guidance from the National Curriculum Council (1992) suggests that music is intended to be a 'flexible subject' and that the programmes of study are designed to allow sufficient flexibility for teachers and pupils to follow their non-western works[30]. Accordingly, adaptation of resources, modification of methods and sensitivity to content can help to ensure the participation of Muslim children in this aspect of the curriculum.

Art in the curriculum is less problematic. The National Curriculum requires that children study the foundation subject of Art up to Key stage 3, i.e. fourteen, as part of an aesthetic experience to develop visual perception and the skills associated with understanding art, craft and design[31]. The Islamic contribution to Art is evident in architecture and design, and Islam encourages the study of Art, but according to certain ground rules:

> these aspects of art which involve human images and iconography are specifically prohibited (Sarwar, p.14).

If these principles are not breached, Muslim children can participate in Art lessons. Therefore, although

> some Muslim pupils may not want to draw human or animal figures... there is a wide variety of artistic expression still available using calligraphic and geometric forms which will allow full development of their artistic skills (Iqra Trust, 1991a, p.13).

At key stages one and two, the development of visual literacy is perceived within National Curriculum documents as inclusive of: the history of art; diverse artistic heritage; and a variety of artistic traditions. Coupled with this is the requirement at key stage three to sustain a chosen idea or theme, investigating and explaining the use of a range of visual resources and exploring how different cultures produce images, symbols and objects. There would thus appear to be ample scope to interpret Art education in such a way as to incorporate cultural diversity[32]. The inclusion of Islamic art, calligraphy and architecture can broaden the curriculum and be of benefit to all children.

In conclusion to this section of curricular needs, there is some concern lest dance, music and potentially art be construed as un-Islamic activities. Mabud (1992) states that whilst neither music nor art is forbidden by Islam, some parental opposition might be met concerning curriculum content. If guidelines are followed, Muslim children may be able to participate, rather than having to be withdrawn. This will depend on the extent to which schools are sensitive to the issues, adapt and modify lessons; and the extent to which Muslim parents feel comfortable with the content and methodology of these aspects of the school curriculum and its organisation.

(iii) General Needs

There are a variety of needs which fall within the organisational management of schools and which concern issues related to schooling in general. We now focus on: home-school links; voluntary-aided status for Muslim schools; single sex schooling; and school governance.

Home-School Links

Enlisting parental support is vital to all attempts to accommodate Muslim needs within the school system. This will be greatly helped if schools recruit Muslim teachers who satisfy national and local regulations, as well as seeking advice from multicultural advisers (Sarwar, 1994; Union of Muslim Organisations, 1989).

> It is sad that even in schools with 90% plus Muslim pupils there are few, if any, Muslim headteachers, teachers, or non-teaching staff. This is often explained away as being due to a shortage of suitably qualified people... positive action should be undertaken to increase the number of Muslim teachers — this could only add to the quality of educational provision (Sarwar, 1994, p.23).

Muslim teachers may perform pastoral as well as academic functions, provide guidance on questions of dress, diet, religion, and explain the nature of the curriculum both formal and 'hidden'[33]. They provide an important source of reference for pupils and may serve as positive role models (McDermott and Ashan, 1980). The Iqra Trust (1991a and 1991b), formed to promote knowledge of Islam in Britain, suggests that home-school links can be fostered by establishing liaison teams in schools with special responsibility for Islamic understanding. A lack of knowledge of the British education system, as well as the language itself, can cause Muslim parents to feel isolated from mainstream school life (Joly 1989). Effective home-school links within the community served by the school is a specific need. Some schools have done a great deal of work on improving communication — as we shall see in chapters 5 and 6. Support for greater and more effective links between schools and parents is strongly endorsed by Muslims and non-Muslims alike. Siraj-Blatchford (1993) comments:

> it needs to be recognised that the key to promoting equality in education is for teachers and educationalists to work *together,* with parents and the community mutually supporting each other in providing children with the most relevant and accessible educational opportunities (p.82).

As evidenced from the discussion so far, effective home-school communications are vitally important opportunities and schools should provide for parents to be informed and consulted, especially on politically sensitive aspects of the curriculum. This would help prevent children being withdrawn from the full curriculum and receiving instead an 'a la carte education' which is neither broad nor balanced.

Voluntary-aided Status

A number of Muslim schools have tried unsuccessfully to obtain voluntary aided status. This would place them in the same category as the more than 7,000 Anglican and Catholic schools, and 21 Jewish institutions which currently receive government funding (Commission for Racial Equality, 1990). Private Muslim schools which boast long waiting lists, increasingly clamour for public funding along the lines presently afforded other denominational schools in Britain (Halstead, 1986; Smith, 1990)[34]. The lobby for voluntary-aided status for Muslim schools, outlined in chapter 1, continues as a struggle for equity in funding[35] and to provide what some Muslim parents feel is the ideal environment to cater for their children's needs. The Education Act (1993) allows for the new possibility of voluntary groups approaching government for funds for establishing and developing their schools[36]. This would open the door to Muslim schools receiving public monies, as other denominational groups have done, albeit on a different basis than voluntary aided. So it may be only a short time before Muslim schools in Britain, founded originally by private contribution, succeed in gaining financial support from the government.

Single Sex Schooling

Parents of both Muslim and non-Muslim backgrounds express a preference for single sex schooling. Although fewer in number than the girls' schools in Britain, Muslim boys' schools are slowly being established. One recent school was founded as a direct result of 'parental concern over the ethos of state schools and the balance and content of the curriculum' (Islamia, 1994, p.6)[37]. The phasing out of single sex schooling by local authorities in the 1970s prompted the formation, in Bradford, for example, of the Muslim Parents Association. The organisation was established to represent the Muslim interest and since then a number of single sex Muslim private schools have been founded in accordance with Islamic principles (Barrell and Partington, 1985). Likewise, the Association for Maintained Girls' Schools was formed because it was feared that single sex schools would dwindle in number[38]. There is some evidence, moreover, that girls perform better academically away from a co-educational environment[39]. Muslim parents express a preference for single-sex schooling, chiefly for girls but also for boys (Anwar, 1982; Mabud, 1992; Iqra Trust, 1991(a))[40]. Some of the co-educational state schools researched for this book have taken the option of single-sex tutoring. This is a practical strategy particularly appropriate for sensitive aspects of the curriculum as discussed earlier in this chapter.

School Governance

Involvement in school governance has been advocated to ensure that the school has a representative view of Muslim interests (Mabud, 1992; Iqra Trust, 1991b). Muslim organisations, for their part, should recognise the important role played by governors in the management of a school and are encouraged to become more proactive in attempting to bring about change within the educational system.

> Although there will almost certainly be a minority on any board of governors, Muslim parents and educationalists should get involved as both elected and co-opted governors ... or LEA representatives (Sarwar, 1994 p.20).

The last few years have witnessed increasing involvement over issues at school and local government levels, notably in London, Birmingham, Leicester and Bradford (Joly, 1989; Nielsen, 1986). The Iqra Trust and

Muslim Educational Trust advocates Muslim participation at all levels of the educational consultative process, to secure a more balanced partnership. Furthermore, Muslim governors should express their views on all matters, 'not just matters relating directly to Muslim parents'; they should participate and become acquainted with education law and procedure (Sarwar, p.21). Clearly the school's link with parents and the community will be vitally important to ensure adequate and effective representation of Muslim issues. This brings into focus the need for effective governor training programmes, to maximise the potential for contribution from and participation by Muslim parents, and others from minority groups in society[41], and to promote effective partnerships in education. Furthermore, it is within school governance that issues like home-school communication and single sex tutoring can be debated, so giving greater opportunity for policy formation.

Conclusion

This chapter has considered the central educational needs of Muslim children as identified by Islamic writers. Three main categories of need have been identified: religious/cultural, curricular and general, with overlap between all areas on the issue of ensuring that each child has access to the curriculum and feels comfortable about participating in school activities. The discussion has incorporated provisions of the National Curriculum and the scope within non-statutory guidance to interpret subjects in a manner which is responsive to Muslim needs. Regular review and update of school policy, especially in the areas of sex and religious education has been highlighted, since these potentially controversial aspects of the curriculum are currently subject to continual change. Further, withdrawal from unacceptable curricula is a legal option, as noted in the discussion, but strategies and initiatives to avoid this right having to be invoked would ensure that schooling does not offer merely an 'a la carte' curriculum which is neither broad nor balanced. Finally, this overview of the educational needs of Muslim children sets out a useful theoretical framework against which to assess the practice of accommodation in British schools, explored in the next chapter.

Notes

1. See 'Prayer Room for One', *British Muslims Monthly Survey,* 1994, 2(2), p.12.
2. *The Education Act* 1944, London: HMSO, ch.31.
3. *The Education Reform Act* 1988, London: HMSO, ch.40.
4. See B. Jowell et al (1989) *British Social Attitudes,* Aldershot: Gower Publishing Company.
5. *The Education Act* 1993, London: HMSO, ch.35.
6. For more on Britain's adoption of the European Convention on Human Rights see R. Beddard (1980) *Human Rights and Europe,* London: Sweet and Maxwell and F. J. Jacobs (1975) *The European Convention on Human Rights,* Oxford: Clarendon Press.
7. *Religious Education and Collective Worship,* Circular No.1/94, London: DFE.
8. As cited in G. Sarwar (1994) *British Muslims and Schools,* London: The Muslim Educational Trust, p.7.
9. For more on this theme see 'Provision of Halal Meat', *British Muslims Monthly Survey,* 2(4), April 1994, pp.3-4; and 'Developments on Halal Meat Control', in which school caterers in Loughborough were praised for their effort in providing a range of halal dishes, *British Monthly Survey,* 1994, 2(5), p.3.
10. See L. Belford (1965) *Introduction to Judaism,* London: Darton Longman and Todd, and E. P. Sanders (1992) *Judaism: Practice and Belief,* London: SCM Press.
11. National Curriculum Council, *Non-Statutory Guidance: Physical Education,* (1992) NCC, York.
12. Education in Turkey assumes a secular ethos, see M. N. Kodamonglu (1965) *Education in Turkey,* Istanbul: Ministry of Education; and A. K. Kazamias (1966) *Education and the Quest for Modernity in Turkey,* London: Allen and Unwin.
13. See 'Changes in School Uniform, Derbyshire', *British Muslims Monthly Survey,* 1993, 1(4), p.10; 'School Uniform Problems, Crawley', *British Muslims Monthly Survey,* 1(10), 1994, p.16; and 'Muslim Girls and School Uniform', *British Muslims Monthly Survey,* 1994, 2(5), p.18.
14. See 'School Uniform Problems', *British Muslims Monthly Survey,* 1993, 1(10), p.16.
15. *Mandla v Dowell Lee* (1983) 1 All ER 1062, HL.
16. *Race Relations Act* 1976, London: HMSO, ch.74.
17. *The Children Act* 1989, London: HMSO, ch.41, and *The Children Act: Guidance and Regulations (1991),* the first third of which contains references to equal opportunities. On this theme see also 'School Forced to take back Rasta brothers', *The Voice,* 1994 May 10, p.4.
18. National Curriculum Council, *Non-Statutory Guidance: Physical Education,* NCC: York, 1992.
19. *Education (No.2) Act 1986,* London: HMSO, ch.61.
20. *Education Act 1993: Sex Education in Schools,* circular number 5/94, London: DFE, 1994.
21. See D. Veasey (1994) 'Sex Education: is its act together?', *Pastoral Care in Education,* 12(2), pp.13-22, June; M. Reiss (1993) 'What are the aims of school sex education?', *Cambridge Journal of Education,* 23(2), pp.125-136 and J. Francis

(1994) 'The Age of Safer Sex', *Community Care,* Jan., pp.18-19; and Children's Legal Centre (1994) 'Sex Education', *Childright,* 105, April, p.7.

22. See Education Act 1993, *Sex Education in Schools,* Draft Circular No. 5/94, section 7, London: DFE, 1994.
23. See 'Sex Lesson Guidelines Condemned', *The Independent,* 15 June 1994, p.2.
24. See 'Section 11 funding', *British Muslims Monthly Survey,* 1994, 2(7), p.31.
25. See also 'New Syllabus for GCSE Islam', *British Muslims Monthly Survey,* 1994, 2(4), p.20.
26. National Curriculum Council: *Non-Statutory Guidance: Music,* York: NCC, 1992, introductory letter.
27. Department of Education and Science: *Physical Education in the National Curriculum,* London: HMSO, 1992; and National Curriculum Council (1992) Physical Education: Non-Statutory Guidance, June 1992, section B3.
28. See 'Mixed Dance Classes', *British Muslims Monthly Survey,* 1994, 2(4), p.22.
29. Department of Education and Science: *Music in the National Curriculum (England),* London: HMSO, 1992.
30. National Curriculum Council: *Non-Statutory Guidance Music,* 1992, section B1.
31. Department of Education and Science: *Art in the National Curriculum,* London: HMSO, 1992.
32. Department of Education and Science: *Non-Statutory Guidance: Art,* National Curriculum Council, 1992, section C7-9.
33. On this theme see 'Drive for more teachers', a new campaign launched by Leicester University to recruit more minority teachers to act as role models, in *British Muslims Monthly Survey,* 1994, 2(3), p.20.
34. See for example attempts made by the Islamia School, London, in 'Islamia School Loses Fight for Voluntary Aided Status', *Asian Times,* 24 Aug., 1993, p.1.
35. I have made this point on a number of occasions see for example, M. Parker-Jenkins (1993a) 'Muslim Rights', *Times Education Supplement,* May 7, p.16.
36. *The Education Act 1993,* London: HMSO, ch.35, section 229-230.
37. See also 'Boys Boarding School Proposed, Sheffield', *British Muslims Monthly Survey,* 2(3), 1994, p.23; and 'Muslim Boys' School, Leicester', *British Muslims Monthly Survey,* 1994, 2(5), p.18.
38. *Times Educational Supplement,* 'Warnock Backs Girls-Only State Sector', 1 March 1991, p.10.
39. See for example, A. Bone (1983) *Girls and Girls-Only Schools: A Review of the Evidence,* London: Equal Opportunities Commission.
40. A recent case in point is local Muslim opposition to the closure of the last two single-sex schools in Bristol; see 'Bristol Single-Sex Schools to Close', *British Muslims Monthly Survey,* 1994, 2(5), p.19.
41. Adequate and effective governor training is an area of particular concern, see 'Asian Governors' Forum', *British Muslims Monthly Survey,* 1994, 2(7), p.31.

Chapter 5

Educational Problems
within the British Context

Theory without a grounding in what is possible in practice is empty;
practice without theoretical guidance is blind (Leicester, 1989, p.41).

The last chapter offered a theoretical perspective on the educational needs
of Muslim children. Discussion now focuses on the perception and
accommodation of these needs by practitioners in Britain[1]. Based on a
twelve month empirical study[2] augmenting earlier work by the author, the
overall purpose of this study was to review the needs, in theory, of Muslim
children and to examine the work being done in British schools to respond
to those needs. This is intended to inform policy-makers, since theory and
practice are complementary, not mutually exclusive. Beginning with a
background description of the study, this chapter examines the results of
the inquiry, highlighting the main issues of concern, and areas of similarity
and divergence in perception between Muslim and non-Muslim headteachers.

Background to the Study

A research team was established with a working brief to identify potential
Muslim and non-Muslim schools, consider issues of access and feasi-
bility, and develop a contract governing relations between the school and

the researcher. Following an initial survey, a contact list of possible schools to include in the research was drawn up. Organisations and individuals were introduced to the study and their levels of interest and involvement gauged. The interview schedules for headteachers were designed in terms of questions clustered around particular themes including school governance; ethnic and religious composition of school personnel; school ethos; and school curriculum. Each interviewee received an introduction, both written and oral, to the project defining its aim: to explore the educational needs of and provision for Muslim children in Britain.

From the outset, schools were selected on criteria based on: the evidence of good practice, obtained from first hand information and referral; the length of establishment of the school; and the willingness of individual institutions to become involved in the research. Furthermore, Muslim and non-Muslim schools were identified within the larger settlement areas of Muslim communities in Britain, detailed in chapter 1, which were found to have considerable experience in meeting the educational needs of Muslim children. Schools were approached to begin the fieldwork phase, 1992-3, with a timetable largely determined by school availability.

After the project had been piloted in three schools, the interview schedules were transcribed and the questionnaires developed and refined accordingly. Local authorities in Leicestershire, Derbyshire and Yorkshire were then contacted in an effort to obtain information concerning more suitable schools to participate in the project. Following this consultation phase, case selection criteria were developed for choosing maintained schools for the study. The schools identified were sent details of the project and their involvement was requested. Schools in Bolton, Bradford and Tower Hamlets were contacted partly to extend the geographical area and partly because Muslim schools were known to have been established in these localities. By selecting both state and Muslim schools from within the same catchment areas wherever possible, it was possible to provide some similarity in units of analysis.

A selection of Muslim schools were also identified, mostly from the author's previous research[3]. They received an interview schedule prepared along the same lines as that for the maintained schools, covering school governance, ethos, staff composition, school curriculum, and academic achievement. The only difference was that the category of questions entitled 'aims of education' was replaced by one entitled 'aims of Islamic education'. This was because a key aspect of the research was to discover the aims of Islamic education, how this is being translated into practice in Muslim schools in contemporary Britain, and what lessons might be learnt for educationalists, especially those of non-Muslim background. Finally, all but one of the Muslim schools were approached, on the basis of previous carefully negotiated access. Re-accessing the institutions was made possible by the care taken to ensure that earlier contracts guaranteeing confidentiality and anonymity were wholly honoured and maintained. Furthermore, publications which emerged were also shared with these schools in the attempt to provide accurate and balanced perspectives. This issue of responsible researching is most important here since access to some of the maintained schools was denied, precisely because of feelings that previous researchers had reneged on agreements of confidentiality and had unfairly besmirched the reputation of the schools in publications. This effectively closed the door on further researchers.

A qualitative research approach was employed in the inquiry and a sample of schools was selected. It was made up of 25% of the private Muslim schools in Britain and an equivalent number of state schools in the inner-city areas of London, Leicester, Bradford, Bolton and Derby. These geographical locations are consistent with the documented settlement patterns of British Muslims noted in chapter 1. The headteachers were the main focus of attention for the study since they were perceived as practitioners who held influential positions. This follows previous research by Joly (1989) which showed that initiatives introduced into schools for the benefit of Muslim children came predominantly from headteachers. In part the interviews were to be used to assess the gap or discrepancies between the theory as espoused by Muslim writers and conceptualised in chapter 4, and to gauge the views of practitioners on the accommodation or neglect of needs. Other methodological techniques used to elicit information were: participant observations of the schools, and analysis of school prospectuses and school records. In the earlier pilot study, teachers, pupils and governors were also interviewed but this book focuses on the responses of headteachers[4]. A semi-structured interview schedule was used with no guidance provided on what the research team had discovered from the initial literature review, incorporating research of Islam, Muslim communities in Britain, voluntary-aided schooling, and the concept of multiculturalism detailed in the previous chapters of this book.

Criteria for selection of the schools was as follows. Of the Muslim schools, institutions were identified, from previous research conducted by the author, which were not transitory in nature and which had been established for a minimum of five years. As documented in chapter 1, the lack of state funding for Muslim schools in Britain since their formation in the 1980s has meant that many have struggled to survive and some have closed. Each of the Muslim schools was to be easily contactable, with a headteacher whom the team considered to be open and co-operative in research. Some of the Muslim schools contacted were wary of public attention and difficult to penetrate, denying access to non-Muslims and outsiders. There were four secondary and two primary schools in the study, each with at least 40 pupils on roll. They demonstrated evidence of good practice, with an established and well-planned curriculum. All the Muslim schools selected were headed by practising Muslims but only one had an all-Muslim staff, the rest depending on non-Muslim teachers to be sensitive and responsive to the Islamic ethos of the institution.

The selection criteria for non-Muslim schools were similarly formulated. A comparative number of state schools were identified, all with over 30-90% of Muslim pupils enrolled. Presently, there are 62 state schools in Britain with a Muslim intake of 90-100%, and 230 with a 75% intake[5]. Again four secondary and two primary schools were chosen for the study, but no single sex boys' school. This is because the majority of Muslim schools established in Britain have invariably been for girls and it was intended to replicate similar situations[6]. Again, headteachers were chosen because they appeared open and co-operative in research, and particular emphasis was placed on identifying schools with evidence of good practice and well-conceived policies of accommodating Muslim children. Many of the schools were recommended by local education authorities in areas with high numbers of Muslim residents. Overall, the children in this study were representative of 37 different countries of origin, the majority of Asian descent; predominantly first generation British Muslim by birth; with a small proportion of second generation British and newly arrived immigrants.

A final note must be added about our methodology regarding access, confidentiality and anonymity. Access was negotiated, and re-negotiated when appropriate, throughout the study. The vast majority of interviews were taped, and a strict code of confidentiality and anonymity applied. (Indeed, permission was even sought for acknowledgements at the beginning of this book.) The headteachers, whether Muslim or not, were interviewed in an atmosphere of non-challenging trust, and the researchers sought to provide scope and opportunity for the Muslim voice to be heard. No individual school or headteacher is cited in the discussion of the results of the study which follows, in line with the guarantee of anonymity[7].

Results of the Study

Both similarities and differences were found between the perceptions of headteachers in state schools and private Muslim schools over Muslim children's needs. Similarity lay in the issue of religion and religious observance, where all interviewees acknowledged religious needs. For example, school dress, provision of prayer room facilities, and flexibility in setting homework for children attending Madrassah or supplementary school in the evenings, were all highlighted as aspects of religion affecting school life. Where the respondents differed was over the *conceptualisation of religion* in the lives of Muslim children. This was described by a Muslim administrator thus:

> ... our education remains the same; it is the total development of the individual. The only difference I can see is that this development takes place in an Islamic environment so our aims also are intellectual, mental, physical, emotional and also spiritual. We do not want to lose sight of the spiritual development of the student. The main purpose is obviously self-realisation and being a Muslim. The ultimate aim is to find out the will of God and [to act] accordingly.

Headteachers of Muslim schools all expressed the need for children to have a spiritual dimension permeating their lives in and out of school. This is understandable, given that the *raison d'etre* of Muslim schools is to promote an Islamic ethos throughout the school and it is consistent with the theoretical perspectives provided earlier. One member of this group described the situation as one where 'all students have the opportunity in

Islamic studies to raise any issues and find out about the Islamic view-point.' This also extended to the issue of identity:

> the general aim of education is to equip this generation for life in [the] future and also to pass onto them the values of the previous generation as well, and this is the aim of education wherever you go but from the Muslim point of view we very much care to maintain their religious identity ... equip them ... to be ... very effective and productive citizens, meanwhile retaining their Muslim identity.

Muslim school headteachers spoke of the importance of faith, prayer, and pride in being a Muslim, which they felt children should be taught, and perceived as the aims of Islamic education, producing ' ... a good Muslim. A good member of the community but most of all a person with a faith. ... to be a person who believes in Islam, practices it and lives by it.' In their view, Islam included moral education and responsibility for the community, whereby 'the world and faith go hand in hand'. Accordingly, children should be taught to be productive British citizens and maintain their Muslim identity. One Muslim headteacher said:

> we find a kind of imbalance in the present system and we are trying to correct the balance so that the individual will be a useful member of society and at the same time be a good follower of Islam.

Conversely, headteachers of state schools saw the religious dimension observances in terms of providing for specific, practical needs of Muslim children rather than fostering a spiritual dimension to their schooling.

There was an interesting response regarding prayer room provision which appeared in the pilot study and in subsequent interviews with headteachers of state schools within the study. The latter group felt the need was not significant and some reported that the prayer room was little used. One state school headteacher said about prayer room provision:

> I feel the reason that there is no pressure from Muslims is because this is a girls' school. I feel that there would be pressure if there were boys present to set up a permanent prayer room especially for the Holy day, Friday, from their fathers. With girls the mothers have a much more domestic approach.

(Confusion and disagreement over whether Muslim girls should pray publicly in the mosque and so need a prayer room in school was highlighted in chapter 2.) Similarly, use of a prayer room appeared sporadic and fluctuated accordingly with one state school headteacher reporting:

> if we have even been asked to make a prayer room available we have always done so and a bowl for washing. We have had requests but we find it fizzles out from their end. I think some adhere to prayer times in the toilets.

Despite the infrequency of use, however, one state school headteacher defended the provision for Friday prayers and prayer room availability:

> there is an acceptance and a tolerance and an acknowledgement that if children want to go to that room on Fridays they can ... so we have actually said if a young Muslim boy comes to you on a Friday, treat it as a genuine request as opposed to giving them the third degree.

Perhaps the issue is not simply one of the availability of a prayer room but also the way in which the system is set up to allow Muslim children to feel comfortable about using it — they might feel under peer pressure not to! Or is the prayer room provision a political statement rather than meeting a personal need? Gender may be a factor here, since boys are more likely to be in the habit of visiting the mosque to pray, and in some communities Muslim girls only pray at home. The study incorporated only girls' schools at secondary level: the use of prayer might be different for boys of this age. Finally, within Muslim schools the role of the headteacher was found to be significant since he/she often assumed responsibility for leading prayer times and pupils witnessed this commitment to the faith. Furthermore, it is understood within the Muslim schools that all children take part in prayer times; it forms an important and normal aspect of the school timetable, so prayer rooms were continually in use.

The largest single need expressed by headteachers of state schools was not religion or religious related needs, as expressed overwhelmingly by heads of Muslim schools. It was the need for *English language acquisition,* recorded from 83% of state school heads — compared with 33% of Muslim school respondents. One state headteacher explained the situation as follows:

> A large majority of our children have language needs that are different in some ways from those of the indigenous population ... we have to take [that] on board in language, that is a very important part of the

89

learning process, and we have to facilitate both the acquisition and the use of language if we are to improve our aims for the children.

Similarly,

> We have a huge percent of Asian children who by definition will be using English less than their peers and therefore are going to under-achieve ... and we also have a huge chunk of kids who have only just arrived in Britain ... it is equivalent of dropping you and me in France as 14 year olds and then saying take your Baccalaureate!

The majority of the Muslim children in this inquiry use English as a second (or third) language and this has profound implications for academic attainment, assessment and testing. Furthermore, the geographical location of the state schools in the study were areas of high ethnic minority settlement, and headteachers commented on the lack of opportunity for their Muslim pupils to interact with indigenous children, further inhibiting their English language competence. Although English language acquisition was not such an important issue for Muslim headteachers, it was acknowledged by some:

> ... there are some girls who have language difficulties but unfortu-nately we do not have the resources to appoint a language support teacher ... nor do we have the facilities for any remedial work ... we are aware of the problems which some of the girls have [but] unfor-tunately we have no means to sort these problems.

Likewise, another Muslim administrator said:

> Most of the girls come from families where the parents are not educated. These girls may not get much guidance and help from their parents and we have to take the role of giving them proper guidance, giving them confidence.

Beyond this the main needs identified were *effective home-school links,* identified by 50% of the headteachers in state schools but only 33% of the Muslim headteachers; and a *balanced curriculum* which was felt to be important by 50% of the state school headteachers and only 16% of Muslim administrators. The issue of *better resources* was not mentioned by state school heads but 83% of Muslim headteachers identified this as a need. This is to be expected given the lack of government funding for

Muslim schools at present. Similarly, *education as a preparation for life* was omitted from responses by state school headteachers, yet 33% of Muslim headteachers felt this to be important. Fifty percent of Muslim headteachers also considered that *racism awareness and monitoring* was a distinct need: this view did not feature among their counterparts in state schools. Finally, *school transportation needs* concerned state school administrators but was not recorded as significant by Muslim school headteachers, a point which will be returned to later in this chapter.

In connection with home-school communication, *teacher awareness* was identified and one state school headteacher said:

> The additional needs of Muslim pupils is for staff to be totally aware of the dynamics of their family situation. Of course there is no typical Muslim family ... but the onus is on us to know about Muslim pupils' backgrounds as completely as possible.

Similarly,

> ... there is a greater need for the teachers to be informed ... I don't think the education needs to be different, I think we need to be sensitive to the different issues which affect the lives of Muslim children.

Another state school headteacher expressed home-school links thus:

> we recognise that the parent is the first educator of the child bringing to school complementary skills and what we are trying to do is work through a sense of partnership and really trying to involve parents in the educational process of their children.

Headteachers of Muslim schools did not perceive the issue of home-school links as being of such paramount importance. This is possibly because the Muslim schools studied were predominantly set within a local and identifiable community in which language and culture were common between the home and school. Trust and co-operation were regarded as having ensured the survival of the private Muslim school based not simply on home-school relations but also on community-school relations in which support from local mosques was significant.. However, one Muslim headteacher noted that the standard of literacy in the family determined whether the parents would be forthcoming in supporting the school; 'the schools can't do everything ... if [the] atmosphere at home is not conducive for the child to work ... to [do] his homework.'

Responses from both categories of headteachers suggested support for a *balanced curriculum*. As discussed earlier in chapter 3, special value is placed in Islam on acquiring knowledge and this was echoed in the responses of the Muslim headteachers:

> Knowledge is very important to Islam, which says that it is important that you do not stay in one place. The Qur'an says that knowledge will bring people higher rank.

Another summed up how this translates into practice:

> As far as the British curriculum ... we make sure that we do not deliver anything that conflicts with the Islamic faith.

Interestingly, in one Muslim school it was said that the responsibility of the school management was 'to bring two cultures together', East and West, and to 'see that both work to realise the aims of the school which is to produce successful students who are able to operate successfully in all cultures'. Likewise, another Muslim administrator said that they tried to straddle the divide, 'to make a bridge to introduce the Muslim community to the West', and to teach and disseminate Muslim knowledge. Accordingly, one Muslim headteacher called for 'objective teaching material as far as Islam is concerned', and another said,

> I don't think the National Curriculum and the Islamic framework are mutually exclusive; on the contrary they can complement each other.

He went on to suggest the need

> to evolve a model of education ... which may not be very much different from the mainstream education in this century ... to retain all the good elements ... and to add the Islamic dimension to that.

It was felt that curriculum should be developed away from an ethnocentric bias, using positive role models and images from Islam, and the Islamic contribution to knowledge made evident. Where curriculum was felt to be unacceptable, some of the state schools in the study provided the opportunity for exemption, although one of the interviewees added:

as a headteacher I have a constant battle to keep the Muslim students within the mainstream while at the same time accommodating their serious needs.

Concerns over the need for a balanced curriculum was also shared by state school administrators. One argued that:

there should be a recognition of the contribution that Islam has made and continues to make to society and a recognition of its contribution to the culture of the world... [Furthermore,] there is a recognition and certainly an acceptance among all [my] staff that where they can, they look for positive role models, for positive pictures of ... black images.

Education as a preparation for life was identified as a need within Muslim schools only:

the most important thing is that we want to educate our students to live in tomorrow's world. I don't want them to live in the past saying Muslim nations did this and Muslim nations did that: what I want them to say is what can we do as Muslims so we can be acknowledged for that good.

The headteacher of one state school identified a problem related to this need:

in school we try to give values so that girls behave responsibly but when they are outside they will encounter irresponsible behaviour and unpleasantness ... it is difficult for Muslim girls who are valued in school but are called racist names out of school.

Public funding for Muslim schools was not specifically requested but the need for *better resources* featured highly, and these would become available if voluntary-aided status was obtained, as discussed earlier in this book. Resources were not identified by state schools, but *improved transport facilities* were mentioned, to enable Muslim children to avail themselves of extra-curricular activities outside the normal school day. Transport was not seen as an issue by Muslim school headteachers, possibly because their schools are normally community schools serving a population within a narrow geographic area. One Muslim headteacher did, however, mention the care that his school has to take in organising extra curricular activities:

we have to communicate to the parents that the girls are going to a safe place, a decent place and the visit would be fruitful [and] we also need a teacher to take responsibility for these girls.

Similarly, a state school administrator explained his situation:

... [some girls] never take part in any outdoor after school activities ... although our Asian kids bring a huge dimension and richness to the school, among the girls there is this whole business of getting back home and getting back safe so there is very little drama, music, dance that they take part in and that's a shame.

At secondary level particularly, state schools serve a wider catchment area and the question of transport is likely to be more problematic, particularly for girls.

Single sex schooling was not highlighted as a major concern, and as noted earlier, some state schools in the study were experimenting in single sex tutoring within a co-educational environment. One Muslim head-teacher commented on this issue:

what is happening in society at large frightens Muslims ... the lack of discipline inside the school also frightens the Muslim and makes him believe that if they have separate or single sex schools their children will be safer ... if the discipline was maintained I don't think the level of aversion to co-education would be the same.

Hindu, Sikh, African-Caribbean and white indigenous parents may also prefer separate schools for girls and for boys, particularly in light of suggestions that single sex education can lead to higher academic attainment[8].

Muslim needs in school diet were seen as being accommodated by a variety of arrangements and were not perceived to be a major difficulty, although the move towards privatisation of school catering provision has caused problems[9]. One state school administrator reported

the catering service is in a sense now a private firm that's won a contract as opposed to the old style — it was your dinner ladies at the school and you had some say about what was happening you know but that isn't really the case anymore.

Nor was the question of school dress regarded as a problem, as all schools in the study designed or adapted uniform in a way that is acceptable to Muslim parents[10]. From the responses of Muslim headteachers specifically, the hijab was seen as demonstrating Muslim identity through attire. It represents the negotiation by Muslims of their position and presence in the British setting; the symbol chosen to preserve identity and clearly the visibility of Islam in schools, whether Muslim and non-Muslim. As detailed in chapter 4, dress has cultural as well as religious significance and not all Muslims share the same view on the appropriateness of dress for females.

Finally, one state school headteacher said she did *not* feel that Muslim children had special needs:

> I would perceive the educational needs to be the same as for all children. I make no sort of separation for the fact that our children come from parents of the ethnic minorities. At the end of the day we have got to prepare children for life and that means living within the social settings that people within Britain live.

Despite her comments, the school in question had spent a great deal of time developing policy to accommodate Muslim children in terms of religion, dress and diet. What her words may suggest is that needs based on purely educational criteria are not dissimilar. All children require preparation for living as an adult within British society.

Conclusion

This chapter has reviewed the empirical research conducted to explore the educational needs of Muslim children in Britain. Headteachers from 25% of the private Muslim schools in the country were interviewed, along with an equivalent number of state school administrators. The interviews were used, in part, to assess the discrepancies between the theory espoused by Muslim writers and the perception of practitioners, both Muslim and non-Muslim, about the accommodation or neglect of needs. Similarities emerged concerning the issue of religion and religious observance but the conceptualisation of religion was different for Muslim headteachers, who felt that a spiritual dimension to a child's education was required that went beyond the rituals of prayer, dress and diet. Conversely, non-Muslim teachers tended to stop short of these religious observances and instead identified an academic issue of critical concern, namely English language acquisition. Whereas *English language needs* was the major concern of state school headteachers, the perceived need within Muslim schools, was a *total spiritual dimension* which the headteachers were attempting to accommodate through school ethos and the curriculum. Problems with language were also felt to be compounded by the fact that the Muslim pupils in question were predominantly learning in their second or third language and living in areas of high ethnic minority settlements with little contact with the indigenous population. Both categories of headteachers identified *effective home-school links* and a *balanced curriculum* as important areas of concern; Muslim headteachers noted *education as a preparation for life*, *improved resources* and *racism awareness* as significant, whereas non-Muslim administrators were concerned with *teacher awareness*; and *school transportation needs.*

It is instructive now to explore the major issues identified in greater depth and within a wider context. The empirical evidence from both Muslim and non-Muslim practitioners in the study also suggests a re-defining of needs in light of the results and a move towards developing a hierarchy of needs which recognises academic as well as religious concerns, and the issue of differentiation among children of the Islamic faith.

Notes

1. I would like to acknowledge the role of Kaye Haw, research assistant to the project for her assistance with fieldwork and in the initial data analysis of the study. See also M. Parker-Jenkins and K. Haw (1995) 'The Educational Needs of Muslim Children in Britain: Accommodation or Neglect?', in S. Vertovec (ed) *Muslims, Europeans, Youth: Reproducing Ethnic and Religious Cultures*, London: Pluto Press.

2. The empirical research for this chapter was conducted as part of a funded project by the University of Nottingham to explore the educational needs of Muslim children in Britain.

3. See for example Parker-Jenkins (1993b) *Educating Muslim Children,* 2nd edition, Nottingham: School of Education, University of Nottingham; and Parker-Jenkins (1991) 'Muslim Matters: An Exploration of the Needs of Muslim Children', *New Community,* 1991, 17(4), pp.569-582.

4. One of the private Muslim schools from this study is currently being researched by myself and two research assistants with financial support from ESRC for an in-depth ethnographic study of the experience of Muslim girls in a Muslim school. Although interviews are being conducted with teachers, governors, and parents, the focus in this instance is on pupil response.

5. *Islamia* (1992) No.18, April, p.2, London: Islamia.

6. Muslim groups founded predominantly single sex schools for girls at the secondary level as highlighted in chapter 1, although increasingly boys schools are being established, see for example, 'Muslim Boys School, Leicester', *British Muslims Monthly Survey,* 1994, 2(5), p.18.

7. In my earlier publications, Muslim schools were deliberately not named but their assistance served to inform my knowledge in the field. This was to ensure confidentiality and anonymity. I am very pleased to say that six years on, the Muslim schools I have been working with are comfortable about being named, as agreed at the beginning of this book, for they richly deserve to be acknowledged for their continued support of my research.

8. For further discussion on this theme see A. Bone (1983) *Girls and Girls-Only Schools: A Review of the Evidence,* London: Equal Opportunities Commission; J. Steadman (1984) 'Examination Results in Mixed and Single Sex Schools', in D. Reynolds (ed) *Studying School Effectiveness,* London: Falmer Press; and R. Deem (1984) *Co-education Reconsidered,* Milton Keynes: Open University Press.

9. See *British Muslims Monthly Survey,* 'Provision of Halal Meat' 2(4), April 1994, pp.3-4; and 'Privateers Bring Taste of Monopoly', *Times Educational Supplement,* Sept. 2, 1994, p.8.

10. Some schools are still experiencing problems over school uniform and the accommodation of religious needs however, see 'Changes in School Uniform', *British Muslims Monthly Survey,* 1993, (1(4), p.10.

Chapter 6

Towards a Needs Hierarchy

> At the end of the day it is the whole child that we are concerned with
> ... [with] part of the child goes the culture, the language and religion
> and what parents feel (headteacher of a state school in the study).

In exploring the educational needs of Muslim children a variety of issues
emerge but particular concerns centre on the nature of the curriculum and
the relationship between home and school. This chapter explores the three
main findings of the study in greater depth, namely: needs revolving
around (i) English language acquisition; (ii) a balanced curriculum; and
(iii) effective home-school links. These are discussed with reference to
theoretical perspectives, and the responses and practical suggestions of
Muslim and non-Muslim headteachers within the study. In drawing out
pupil needs associated with 'culture, language and religion' and with
'what parents feel', the discussion moves on to developing a needs
hierarchy to assist teachers in identifying needs, assessing the extent of
accommodation thus far; and providing a practical framework against
which to consider development or modification of school policy and
practice.

From this study into the educational needs of Muslim children, it is
evident that some concerns have been addressed thus far. Structural
changes in the school system have ensured that school diet, school dress,

99

physical education and prayer rooms have to some extent been accommodated by policy initiatives instigated in the 1970s and 1980s. This reflects Jeffcoate's view that

> good multicultural education should be sensitive to 'special needs' and make special provision in terms of language, religion, diet and dress (1981, p.32).

These accommodations have been based on local and individual school effort and the findings are consistent with the documented initiatives of local education authorities, particularly in areas with sizeable numbers of minority ethnic groups (Nielsen, 1986). This study suggests that needs highlighted in category one of the theoretical framework — that is religious/cultural needs (discussed in chapter 4) — are by and large accommodated by headteachers as those which can most easily be addressed by the school within the confines of their own institutions. There are varying levels of adherence to any faith and Muslim parents and children demonstrate a spectrum of needs on the issue of dress, diet and prayer. The schools in the study have responded practically in this instance with a variety of initiatives ranging from adaptation of school dress to the provision of prayer rooms.

Furthermore, these initiatives are perceived as expressions of 'goodwill' in a balancing act which aims to delay if not omit the accommodation of those needs described in categories two and three, that is curricular and general needs, which are the possible minefields that multicultural/anti-racist policies have thus far failed to address. Lacking uniformity in provision and progression, these initiatives, note Troyna and Williams (1986), and Troyna and Ball (1987), demonstrate significant differences in the way concepts such as 'education for equality', and multicultural/anti-racist education have been conceived and implemented by individual schools and localities. Moreover, while there was some opportunity for initiatives by schools and education authorities prior to the *Education Reform Act,* (ERA)[1], the post 1988 era has witnessed a gradual shrinking of space available for schools to continue innovative ways of responding to cultural diversity in the classroom. Troyna and Selman (1989) have concluded on this point:

in the likely absence of further initiatives along anti-racist lines at ERA level the responsibility for change lies more than ever at the chalkface (p.35)

Key areas of need which remain do not concern the practical everyday aspects of school life, such as school dress and diet, but rather are concerned with academic attainment. *English language acquisition,* a *balanced curriculum* and *effective home-school links,* which featured significantly in the study, all revolve around academic concerns of progression and success.

(i) English Language Acquisition

In the study, English language acquisition was considered the major area of concern by state school administrators. One headteacher explained the background differentiation of Muslim pupils and what he saw as a cause of the problem:

> With our Pakistani community ... a sizeable proportion are second generation ... and in a few cases third, but our Bengali community is very much first generation which makes a difference in needs in many ways.

He went on to assess the situation thus:

> ... it is really the acquisition of English language [for] the children. Many of our children who come to us from three into our receptions ... are still very much immersed in their own mother tongue, be it Panjabi or Bengali.

Similarly, another headteacher commented:

> I certainly feel that the language acquisition is important, from the point of view of the school there is [a] big emphasis on the play situation to actually facilitate language acquisition especially in the schools such as my own, where the playground languages are very much Bengali or Panjabi and the only sense where the children have anything like ... a fairly standard form of English is through the interaction that they have with the teachers.

Another state school administrator noted the effect of immigration on his school district and the subsequent issues relating to school immersion:

101

the pattern of immigration has been that the Sikhs and Hindus have been here longer and the Muslims are the ones in fact who are still arriving. If a new youngster arrives she or he will invariably be from Pakistan so it is a much newer stage of integration.

This clearly has implications for assessment of language, as one state school administrator noted:

> some of our children ... had only come to us three, four terms before we were SATing them, still very much immersed in their own mother tongue.

In terms of practical solutions to improving English language acquisition, a variety of strategies were being employed by schools in the study. One institution reported:

> we are very conscious of the language needs of our students. We have a whole school spelling policy and reading schemes to target those students with special needs especially the Asian students.

Another strategy used to tackle language was suggested by a state school administrator in the study who took the view that as well as children, no parent should be asked to cast off their language before coming into school[2]. Accordingly,

> [here] you would come into school to find parents working alongside their own children in bringing their expertise and knowledge of the child into the learning situation but also from their own point of view developing themselves as people i.e. through the English language baby clinic, borrowing libraries and things of that nature.

The Swann Report (1985) on the education of children from ethnic minority groups concluded that British society was not providing equality of opportunity and saw multicultural/anti- racist teaching as applicable to all schools in all areas. With regard to language, the Report preferred specialist help to be provided within mainstream schooling rather than withdrawing pupils. Another issue to emerge from this debate concerned support given to a pupil's mother tongue. Corner (1988) argues on this point:

> the overall evidence from modern research is that bilingual and bicultural children, if they are encouraged to attain a reasonable

degree of balance between the language and cultures, develop an enhanced intellect. (p.7).

As evidenced in this study, home-learning is very much a feature of Muslim family life. Children are taught language, religion and culture by parents or in a madrassah. Supplementary education is an aspect of life of various minority groups although some supplementary schools operate to improve academic attainment, rather than transmitting cultural and religious values (Brock and Tulasiewicz, 1985)[3]. In one of the state schools in the study, six languages were being offered, including Urdu, Panjabi and Hindi, to respond to the belief that mother tongue languages have a legitimate place within the curriculum. As Dabene (1993) states 'access to the dominant language should not lead to confinement in a closed universe' (p.248).

> A significant principle of education for a multicultural society is that it should afford the different ethnic groups equality of educational opportunity (Jeffcoate, p.4).

Muslim children will not realise their true potential if they lack written and oral competence. *Diversity of languages* should be considered not as a deficiency but as an asset (Squelch, 1993). This should be emphasised governmentally and institutionally. English language as the medium of instruction in British schools clearly has an important place, but 'opportunities need to be created for various groups to learn their own language because of its cultural importance' (ibid, p.45). The matter of parity of languages is also an issue, as Dufour (1990) observes:

> in a multicultural Britain as well as a European Britain, some facility in a minority language such as Gujarati or Punjabi, for white and black children, has an equal claim to relevance as a facility in a modern European language (pp.125-126).

Indeed, this study demonstrates that Muslim children have often learnt two or three languages: their mother tongue, community languages, and Arabic for Qur'anic instruction, before tackling English. In terms of academic performance within the school, however:

> students who have a *limited proficiency in the language of instruction* are at most risk of failing and dropping out of school because they

103

have not mastered the language required to cope with the learning material (ibid).

The challenge for teachers lies in meeting the language needs of pupils who are required to study through a medium which is not their first language (Ellis, 1985; McLaughlin, 1987; Lightbown and Spada, 1993), and which is critical for success as conceived by the National Curriculum and its associated attainment targets. The second challenge lies in government meeting these needs, which it has endorsed through European undertakings, and which carry clear implications for resourcing and teacher education. (This theme will be developed further in chapter 7.)

Second language acquisition should not act as a barrier against attainment but this accommodation of need will require increased financial support and resources. This is particularly significant in the present climate, when section 11 funding is vulnerable and under threat. Introduced in 1966, this financial provision was made available by the Home Office mainly to help immigrant children learn English and has been a mainstay for schools attempting to respond to language needs of pupils (McMahon and Wallace, 1993). Two questions arise:

— are Muslim children receiving equality of opportunity through existing arrangements for English language acquisition in British state schools? and

— what is this likely to imply in terms of equality of outcome?

Clearly, the next phase of responding to needs requires more than tinkering with educational structures. Concerted effort is required to ensure that Muslim children, and those of other minority groups, are not disadvantaged due to what is fundamental to academic performance, that is familiarity with and success in the English language. This is not to diminish the value of the first language or community languages, but to give urgency and legitimacy to developing an educational system which is responding to the linguistic requirements that help determine academic success and future access to the labour market. What is required is a broad school policy on language, which places value on different language and dialectic abilities, includes consideration of community languages and provides support to improve and enhance language competences.

(ii) A Balanced Curriculum

> ... the curriculum is not ours anymore ... the curriculum is a National
> Curriculum and I don't feel [it] reflects the level of sensitivity ... that
> is the part we try to build in not just for Muslim children but for all
> faiths practised in this school (state school headteacher in the study).

When asked whether schools were able to provide an Islamic perspective
to curricular offerings, both Muslim and non-Muslim headteachers interviewed in the study highlighted the difficulties inherent in negotiating the
present National Curriculum and incorporating an appropriate level of
cultural diversity, let alone an Islamic dimension. Their responses also
outlined what they were doing to deal with this tension.

One state school headteacher highlighted the problems experienced
with the current National Curriculum thus:

> the agendas in schools are not set by schools ... they are set nationally
> and they have to be managed locally and within ... schools and that
> does generate problems ... and the other main issue is that the national
> agendas are not constant — they are continuously changing agendas
> and ... we just have to implement the change ... To make sure that we
> respond to the National Curriculum in a creative way and don't disrupt
> student learning, and actually optimise student outcomes within this
> changing context, hasn't been easy.

Another administrator in this group argued 'our ability to change the
curriculum is now minimal because it is now centrally driven'. He cited
one situation in which he had been particularly interested in focusing on
career options for Muslim girls, but where curriculum change and financial restraints on links with industry had effectively brought the work to
an end.

Another headteacher likewise contrasted the pre-1988 and post-ERA
period:

> ... within history for example we have a big input — we do the Islamic
> contribution to medicine. Now with the National Curriculum there is
> the constraint of having to do the history of Britain as a compulsory
> larger element but the staff are happy to be able to include the
> contribution of Islamic culture to the world in the choice section ...

With particular reference to the needs of Muslim children, one state school administrator responded with the query:

> is the curriculum developed to [provide] an Islamic orientation? That's a good question ... I would have said at one time we were very sensitive to ... our community and to the experiences that our children were experiencing both ... within their homes ... and their parents' home backgrounds, and I was more than happy with the general direction that the school was going in.

He went on to elaborate using history teaching as an example:

> For instance from a sense of history, history would be taken from the child and traced back through parents, through grandparents ... I think with the advent of the National Curriculum in some ways it has actually reverted our curriculum and experiences very much into monosyllabic terms.

The impact of the National Curriculum was also felt when children visited their parents' homeland:

> the school is affected by children ... returning either to Bangladesh or Pakistan for quite lengthy times. Now in the past we viewed this as a very positive experience which children could come back and share with us. I don't know whether the National Curriculum has taken this one on board ... because certainly now children are missing huge chunks of the National Curriculum through being back in their parents' own countries ... so I think very generally from the question asked I would say that our children have got a lot of abilities ... whether the actual SAT results show them in the best light is debatable.

As might be expected, no state school headteacher reported a total Islamic dimension to the curriculum. They reported a fragmented approach whereby staff looked for positive role models and materials to assist teaching. A recognition of the contribution that Islam has made to world culture was mentioned and, generally, a willingness by staff to seek out the opportunity to incorporate an appropriate Islamic orientation. For example, work on Islamic patterns within mathematics teaching and the Islamic contribution to science were being developed within lessons.

Conveying to parents the nature and rationale of the National Curriculum was also mentioned. One headteacher from a state school described his efforts in this regard:

> a group of parents actually came to me about October time to ... say why are you teaching the Vikings to our children? They don't seem to know very much about it, why are we doing these things? I mean I think the pat answer would be because it is part of the National Curriculum ... [but] what we decided to do was ... to get the National Curriculum attainment targets in history and translate them into Bengali and Urdu and to actually display these around the upstairs hall.

To explain their objections more fully, the staff then involved parents in the learning experience:

> in addition to that we got samples of children's work and artefacts. We looked at various areas and tied them up with the attainment targets in history and then invited parents to come and share an experience with us. So we were using Victorian ... artefacts [and] with that the parents started to get some idea of what it was the National Curriculum was saying other than ... presenting them with a book or a statement. It meant more to them because they were being run through the same experiences as we would want the children to actually ... go through, the actual process of first hand concrete experience.

This is another example of schools trying to tackle what is perceived as a monocultural curriculum with parents of diverse backgrounds.

Finally, positive ways of looking at current curriculum in one state school visited, revealed that they had tried to look at sections of the National Curriculum and use them as a springboard to engender those experiences that children bring to school. For example, the Hindustanis were incorporated into the curriculum as an example of an ancient civilisation and with which many of their parents could identify. So although they said that opportunities to use the personal experience of the children within teaching had diminished substantially since enactment of the Education Reform Act, this school was still trying to continue using individual experience and using the community as a resource. Striking the right balance is particularly difficult, however, as one state school head-teacher remarked:

> the exams at 16 plus are set by the exam boards and if we were to have too much deviation from the National Curriculum we would actually disadvantage our students and that disadvantage in turn would be published and we would come out as a school that isn't achieving, and then there is nothing in the mainstream system that will acknowledge alternative achievement.

Responses from Muslim headteachers were similar in that an imbalance in the National Curriculum was identified, but this was offset by staff in Muslim schools looking for the scope to incorporate an acceptable Islamic dimension. All the Muslim schools in the study were teaching the National Curriculum, selecting options which provided the opportunities for development along Islamic lines and trying to avoid unacceptable curricula. One headteacher noted that:

> the educational needs don't suffer because Islam actually supports learning actively so ... one can argue from within Islam. One doesn't sort of challenge it from outside and say that Islam is holding children back — it doesn't. We have got to understand the context of the children and actually respond to it.

Another administrator from this group stated:

> I don't think that the National Curriculum and the Islamic framework are mutually exclusive; on the contrary they complement each other. ... when we select the topics we keep the community needs in mind and we have found the integrated humanities quite useful.

Muslim headteachers stated that their staff identified subject matter within specific lessons that could have relevance to Islam or the school community. The curriculum was being used to challenge stereotypes, particularly regarding the academic potential of Muslim girls, and to explore the issue of Islamic identity and responsible citizenship in Britain. Although the issue of imbalance in the curriculum was recognised by Muslim schools in the study, they found it less problematic, since their private status gave them the freedom to develop curriculum according to their needs. They had certainly sought to work to the National Curriculum but avoided compromising their religious convictions. Some of these institutions made concerted efforts to introduce the Islamisation of knowledge (outlined in chapter 3) within an educational framework which also accommodated the demands of the National Curriculum.

A curriculum, national or otherwise, needs to reflect a balance of perspectives, incorporating the achievements and contributions of cultural groups. Indeed Lawton (1980) defines curriculum as 'a transmission of the culture'. But whose culture is being transmitted? Reviewing the national curriculum documents implemented since ERA, they appear at best Eurocentric and at worst Britocentric but rarely multicentric. A movement away from what Leicester (1989) describes as seeing education 'through ethnocentric spectacles' (p.42) would require a deliberate shift from this bias. Notwithstanding the perceived strait-jacket of the National Curriculum, there are possibilities to acknowledge the contributions to knowledge by Islam and from all over the world, and to broaden the received canon of knowledge.

Finding the right balance between the indigenous and minority cultures as expressed in the curriculum continues to be an area of concern. It is no longer possible to make the school curriculum responsive and sensitive to Islam without simultaneously negotiating the National Curriculum. Recently, the *Dearing Report* has recommended that the British national curriculum be reduced by about a third, which provides greater freedom for curriculum innovation in other subject areas[4]. By attempting to seize the initiative and using the newly created space to develop an appropriate Islamic dimension to subject areas at relevant key stages, schools could compensate for previous omissions. Without commitment to do so, this aspect of multicultural teaching will be jeopardised or sacrificed for the dictates of an homogenised, ethnocentric curriculum[5]. (This issue is discussed further in chapter 7.) The National Curriculum also prescribes certain standard assessments. There are implications for pupils whose background is disregarded and they may face external examinations which incorporate questions on unacceptable curricular areas[6]. If schools respond sensitively to national assessment, there are benefits to be gained for both Muslim and non-Muslim children:

> the achievement of respect for others lies in knowledge — the concept of respect for self is achieved in a similar way (McGee, 1992, p.18).

The next phase of needs moves beyond practical, structural changes in the school system and strikes at the heart of educational policy in this country and the implementation of a National Curriculum. Eggleston (1990) considers these policies to be assimilationist in nature, clearly demonstrated by the National Curriculum documents which make compulsory certain British or Eurocentric topics and shift alternatives to the Western perspective predominantly into options which can be followed or ignored. In the post-ERA era, only very committed schools have ensured that the move towards an ethnocentric curriculum has been resisted. Responses from headteachers in this study have demonstrated how difficult it has become to retain a multicultural perspective within the curriculum. One headteacher of a state school described the overall objective thus:

> ... we try not to give offence to any one group in ... a mixed race/mixed cultural school ... we build in a sensitivity to the religious/cultural norms that our children are being raised by. So it is not just an Islamic orientation. I think it is a sensitivity to Hinduism, to Sikhism, to teaching.

(iii) Effective Home-School Links

This study raised an issue among state school headteachers, not simply over making home-school links but also ensuring *effective* communication between parents and teachers. The successful education of all children depends on the co-operation, mutual understanding and communication between the home and school, and in the case of pupils from culturally diverse groups this is doubly important, in order to diminish misunderstanding, mistrust or anxiety and to assist in raising the academic attainment of pupils. Muslim headteachers in the study were not negligent but they did not have the same problem. Their schools were normally located within a community with which they were familiar linguistically, religiously and ethnically, whereas state school administrators recognised their limitations and the concerted efforts needed to bridge a gap between home and school.

One state school administration noted the different educational backgrounds of parents and efforts to improve home-school communication thus:

the learning experience of children is not shared by parents. What the children are experiencing is very different from what their parents experienced and in ... partnership with parents we increasingly have to ... tell the parents what it is the children are doing, how it is being assessed, and the whole concept of the National Curriculum attainment targets and levels of attainment are totally alien to a large majority of our parents as they would be I think, to the English parents as well.

Another administrator in this category admitted that:

a big weakness is our home-school liaison. The Muslim community is not well represented on bodies like our home parent association. Parents evenings and fund raising events are generally supported by the Muslim community but it is mainly the fathers.

To help parents feel welcome in the school, a number of strategies were employed by the headteachers. In one institution, a 'parents' room' was set aside offering hospitality and a place to belong: it was felt that neither classrooms nor staffrooms are places where parents feel particularly comfortable. Other schools in the study recognised the value of using the community as a resource, to operate an open door policy and to explain fully to parents what is happening in the school whenever necessary. One state school headteacher saw his role as:

to look at common themes where both parents and school can work together. How we might support this within a home context ... I am fully convinced that the way forward and perhaps the only way forward is where [the] school is working in conjunction with the home and with the general community in trying to actually share their complementary sort of skills and experiences ... I think the school is making valuable inroads into trying to latch on to the things familiar, that are meaningful to parents, teachers and children in the fact of trying to raise the achievements and the self-concept of children that we care for.

Teacher contact with the home was likewise noted by another state school administrator who said: 'you will also find that members of staff go to the homes of pupils for meals and things such as this.'

The question of home-school links is potentially problematic because of the various interpretations of what is permissible within Islam. In terms of liaising with the local community, one headteacher of a state school with 96% Muslim children on roll had this to say:

> there are something like five main mosques in the area ... and then in addition to these there are a number of satellite, you wouldn't call them mosques but certainly satellite and supplementary schools.

This school is used for mother-tongue teaching in the evening, it runs homework groups for children after school, and a Bengali Saturday school operates on its premises. The headteacher used this forum for establishing contacts with local representatives and Imams:

> we met informally in many ways to say initially, what do you want for your children and how might [the] school be able to accommodate your wishes?

Further contact was made with Imams from the five main mosques in the area. Muslim assembly was held at school once a month for all the children and each of the five Imams came in to conduct the assembly on a rota basis. Another state school administrator told how he was learning Urdu to ease the language barrier:

> what has been helpful is that I am able to have a collection of words and phrases for kids ... some of the brighter older kids are teasing me frantically ... its interesting because I have heard now from a few of our Muslim parents ... Mr. ___ is learning our language!

He felt the overall benefit of having some familiarity with Urdu out-weighed any risk of seeming to patronise: rather it made a statement about his attempts to glean an insight into his pupils' world. Another state school headteacher had a slightly different approach to involving parents:

> We make sure that parents' evenings have interpreters and we have our staff that includes the whole range of community languages. We invite other people to come in and out as interpreters for parents evenings and increasingly the level of participation is improving. And we find that the learning of children improves when the parents are actually involved. So we have a very active parent-teacher associ-ation.

Part of this school's policy was to be sensitive to issues which affected Muslim children, such as supplementary education:

a number of children go to the mosque in the evenings and we have to work out with parents how much time they have for doing their homework ... and it does need a partnership between parents and teachers rather than looking on it as a disadvantage.

As we saw in chapter 3, the vast majority of Muslim children between the ages of 5 and 13 attend mosque schools in the evenings, for Qur'an instruction[7]. Teachers should take account of this when determining school policy on homework.

There is an abundance of literature on the issue of home-school links and many theorists are critical of some schools' poor record in this aspect of schooling. Writers are clear that ethnic minority parents must not be isolated because of difficulties in communication. Corner (1988) observes that many of the educational problems which we may now see as 'ethnic minority problems' are in fact longer term problems previously suffered by many Europeans, and that these often lie within the educational system itself, rather than in the family. There is a danger, states Macbeth (1989), of equating ethnic minority families with disadvantage, whereas varying degrees of disadvantage exist in minority and majority groups alike. Wolfendale (1992) and Tomlinson (1984) emphasise that separate home-school policies for ethnic minority families would be separatist and ultimately racist. What they suggest is that the distinctive needs of pupils from ethnic minority backgrounds should be seen as 'temporal and transitional' (p.97). Wolfendale maintains that:

we can work within the frameworks of different models of parental partnership in general to ensure the maximum participation of all parents. On the basis of equal opportunities, we can apply differential strategies sensitively to draw in parents who were educated in other countries, whose first language may not be English and who, above all, need to feel welcome in and be welcomed into the formal institution of school (ibid).

Barriers to equitable parental participation is described by Vassen (1986):

Lack of involvement has three main strands. First, the unwillingness of teachers to participate with parents who are regarded as 'nonprofessionals' and thereby not qualified to offer anything. Second, the notion that parents' duties cease at the school gate. Third, the schools' rigidity in structuring visits that do not take into account the work commitments of parents (p.131).

Discussing the involvement of Muslim parents specifically, Macleod (1985) also identifies three specific concerns. Firstly, difficulties caused in home-school communication because English is often not the parents' first language; secondly, the shortage of teachers from minority ethnic groups; and thirdly, that parents from different religious, linguistic and cultural backgrounds often view schools differently from indigenous parents. Tizard, Mortimore and Burchell (1988) add that differences revolve especially around expectations about particular issues such as the role of punishment and the emphasis that should be given to formal education. They declare that:

> we do not underestimate the difficulty of explaining modern teaching aims and methods to parents from a very different culture. Nor do we suggest that teachers should — or indeed would — accede to parental wishes which were totally at variance with their own approach. But unless schools are prepared to discuss such issues with parents, explain their approach, listen to parents' points of view, and go some way towards meeting them, they cannot hope to enlist parental support for their work (p.80-81).

Impediments to effective home-school relations need thus to be overcome. Research has been conducted to explore the involvement of minority ethnic group parents, and the frequent finding, notes Marland (1983) is that they include 'a rather high proportion of non-visitors to the school', which has frequently been taken by teachers to denote apathy (p.2). He refutes this assumption, arguing instead:

> the reasons, however, were *not* those of the apathetic; rather they are largely the practical problems of shift hours, language difficulties, and the fact that school is often the only major 'white' institution with which an Asian in an English city has to relate (ibid).

A further issue is the assumption of disadvantage. As in all groups there may be levels of disadvantage but:

models of disadvantage may also be ethnocentric, and professionals from white middle-class backgrounds may denigrate minority child-rearing patterns and parental behaviour. Teachers working within the disadvantage model may come to view their work more in a social-pastoral care context than an examination-oriented or skill-oriented one; schools for the disadvantaged are not places where high academic achievement is expected. Teachers' views may thus clash with the expectations of minority parents, who do expect their children to achieve examination passes or acquire skills that will be vocationally useful (Tomlinson, 1984, p.118).

This point is echoed by Akhtar (1993) in *The Muslim Parents' Handbook* which cites underachievement of their children as a major concern of Muslim parents.

Legislation in the 1980s extended and improved parental rights with regard to their children's education, incorporating: choice in schooling; information on schools; annual reports; pupil progress; school sanctions; and parent involvement in school governance[8]. There is thus a legal obligation on all schools within the state system to provide parents with information pertaining to these issues. As an extension of this concept, notes Sarwar (1994), it is helpful to provide information in a way that can be understood and in appropriate community language;

> headteachers should be asked to ensure that information booklets for parents should contain all the information relevant to their children (including the right of withdrawal, school meals, holidays, changing, showering and sportswear). These should be translated into the appropriate languages when necessary. (p.7).

There is a *two-way need* for accurate information:

> problems always crop up when preconceived notions and a lack of knowledge produce extreme opinions and the doors of consultation close. Sadly, this is often the case with the authorities (headteachers and LEA officials) when it involves Muslim pupils and their parents. We have to acknowledge that in our British society there is a marked lack of factual knowledge about Islam and Muslims, resulting in many ill-founded fears about them. It is time for bridges of understanding to be built for the greater benefit of our society (ibid).

115

In order to facilitate greater awareness and understanding between schools and minority parents, Tizard et al (1988) argue for a multicultural approach in which parents have the opportunity to contribute knowledge of their culture and about their children to the teachers; equally, teachers need to be given the space to explain their methods and aims to parents. As part of a twelve stage programme to improve home-school relations, Macbeth (1989) includes: a system of welcome at all times for schools; termly class meetings; parent accountability to teachers; and a system of home-visiting.

Of particular interest to this discussion is home-school liaison. Should this be a specialist function of the school, especially in light of language difficulties or should it be generalist? There is clearly a place for inter-preters in schools with a high percentage of ethnic minority pupils and for translating school publications and written communications into appro-priate languages. However, if home-school visits are left entirely to one or two link teachers in the school, there is the danger that all teachers will not have the opportunity to gain greater insight and knowledge about the children's backgrounds. If all teachers have regular contact with parents, home-school communication would not be simply someone else's respon-sibility: 'the very presence of a home-school liaison teacher on pastoral care staff may be a barrier to genuine educational partnership' (ibid, p.169). A combination of generalist and specialist approaches to home-school structures could provide a more effective system.

During the last few years new developments in home-school links include the notion of assessing school performance in terms of parental involvement and including such activities as one indicator of school effectiveness[9]. School 'partnership' comes at a time when expectations of accountability and quality assurance within schools have increased. This is in keeping with OFSTED requirements that inspection teams take note of the extent of a school's parental and community involvement and the views of parents[10]. School contracts are another development, in which schools and parents set out the expectations and responsibilities each expects of the other. Some models include pupils as a third category. Though without legal authority, these contracts or agreements can be useful in setting out expectations, intents and shared responsibilities and are being enacted elsewhere in Europe also (Jones et al, 1992). Based on the notion of educational partnership, such two- and three-way contracts are currently being considered as models of good practice. It is hoped that they are a way forward, signalling parental involvement and reciprocal responsibilities which should culminate in educational provision in the child's best interest[11].

In short the traditional narrow concept of parent involvement is beginning to shift. Not only must the role of gender and social class bias preventing the involvement in all parents (Banks, 1989) be recognised but a broader view is required of the role of parents, a view that includes those who are illiterate or not proficient in the school's language of instruction (Squelch, 1993)[12]. Clearly, these suggestions will require a change in school culture towards flexibility in the timing of meetings and an overhaul of structures currently restricting school-parent interaction: a movement away from parents as fund-raisers to parents as partners. This will demand time, energy and resources, so as to develop a system of home-school communication which reaches out and attempts to include all parents.

Towards a Needs Hierarchy

The focus of the discussion in this chapter has been on the key areas of concern emerging from the empirical study, namely: English language acquisition; a balanced curriculum; and effective home-school links. It adds to the theoretical perspectives provided by Islamic writers, described in chapter 4, and indicates a requirement to broaden and re-define the concept of need. In assessing the needs of Muslim children and recognising the potential for wide differentiation within this group, as highlighted throughout the book, a framework for needs analysis is helpful. Consideration of the following issues permits understanding of: overall progress; areas of accommodation; areas of neglect; and identification of needs to be adopted or modified within school policy. Each school is unique in its requirements but this framework could enable educators to begin to assess their progress in their schools, to prioritise issues and move towards developing a hierarchy of needs tailored to their own institution.

At the outset educators can obtain an overall perspective of the school situation by asking:

— What needs have been accommodated so far?

— What needs are being expressed? and

— By whom?

— Are they gender issues?

— Are the needs generational? (are pupils British-born? were their parents? or are they newly arrived?)

— Are socio-economic factors relevant?

In the absence of expressed demands by Muslim parents or communities, educators can obviously still seize the initiative and develop policy to enhance educational provision and experience. After conducting their initial survey, educationalists can utilise the three categories, discussed in chapter 4 and now expanded in light of the findings described in chapter 5, to explore issues in greater depth. Although not an exhaustive list, examples of good practice cited in previous chapters are incorporated within this framework. Further, whilst this needs analysis has emerged out of inquiry into the educational needs of Muslim children, many of the issues raised have application for other pupils.

A Framework for Needs Analysis

Categories of Needs

i) Religious/cultural
This category of need requires consideration of:

— school dress code

— school policy on hair for male and female pupils

— physical education dress

— school diet

— collective acts of worship

— prayer room provision

— fasting periods

— school activities during fasting

— alternative rooming during lunchtime fasting

— religious holidays

— Friday prayers

ii) Curriculum

In negotiating the National Curriculum on behalf of the school, areas of need include:

— balance
— global perspective
— a multicultural permeation model reflected in all subject areas
— recognition of cultural and linguistic accomplishments of ethnic minority groups
— an appropriate Islamic perspective
— promotion of positive images
— avoidance of tokenism
— avoidance of bolted-on dimension of minority achievements
— access to resources of minority groups
— using the community as a resource
— multiculturalism/anti-racism embedded in the 'hidden curriculum'

iii) Linguistic

This category of need requires consideration of:

— the level of English language competence
— support for English language acquisition
— mother tongue competence
— community languages accomplishments
— support for mother tongue and community languages
— languages offered at GCSE level
— a school language policy

iv) General

This category of need requires consideration of:

— a genuine commitment to a multicultural/anti-racist policy for the whole school
— care over pronunciation of children's names
— adoption of an anti-harassment policy, which tackles racist and religious abuse

— pastoral support for victims of abuse

— safety bases or areas of safety in the school grounds for bullied children to go

— single sex groupings within a co-educational context

— effective home-school links

— parents-teacher associations

— translations of school communications

— home-school visits

— home-school liaison tutors

— termly class meetings

— cultural awareness about all groups

— in-service teacher training

— school contracts incorporating parental accountability

— written reports and consultations

— a parents' room in the school

— structures for pupil representation

— homework policy that accommodates attendance at supplementary school

— a representative governing body

v) **Individual**

Beyond these religious/cultural, curricular and general needs affecting all children, there may be

— further special needs pertaining to an individual child.

While educationalists must respond sensibly and sensitively to group needs, it is important to recognise the requirements of the individual child, as in any sound educational philosophy. There is no such thing for example, as *the* Muslim child — as if he or she typifies all the needs and desires of all Muslim children. Nor should individual children within a group, which has a collective identity, be given a label which is generally applied. Bangladeshi children are a case in point, overshadowed by reports of underachievement: reports that are currently being challenged by Bangladeshis who have achieved educational success[13]. There is also no one stereotypical Muslim child who embraces all the characteristics of a religious group member; hence the title of this book, *children* of Islam. As we saw in chapter 1, Muslims are not a homogeneous group, all sharing the same linguistic, cultural and socio-economic backgrounds. Rather, Muslims are divided along national, political, sectarian lines with no common consensus over how religious adherence translates into everyday life. Muslim children are from diverse cultural backgrounds and have both shared experience*s and* individual needs. A group identified as 'different' is often assumed to be internally homogeneous, even when this is clearly not the case: there is a danger that discussions of ethnicity seek to impose stereotypic notions of 'common cultural needs' upon heterogeneous groups with very different social aspirations and interests (Brah, 1992).

Within the framework of needs' analysis above, individual as well as group needs can be more systematically determined. Informed by the good practice evidenced in the study and constructed and developed in light of the individual school situation, the framework can serve as a helpful model in identifying areas of concern and as a starting point for moving towards policy aimed at enhancing provision for Muslim children and other pupils within each educational setting.

Conclusion

In examining the educational needs of Muslim children within a British context, this study highlighted three main areas of concern: English language acquisition, a balanced curriculum and effective home school links. There was a discrepancy in perception between what the Islamic writers cited as legitimate needs, as discussed in chapter 4. Explanation for this may lie in the *level* of concern over spiritual matters rather than suggesting that these theorists lack concern over academic performance[14]. Questions raised in the study focused on a) the general needs applicable to all Muslim children, such as school dress, diet, prayer room provision; b) a balanced curriculum; c) specific academic needs resulting from socio-economic background and particularly linguistic concerns; and d) individual needs as people in their own right. A needs analysis framework was proposed, setting out these categories and providing redefinition and expansion of needs for assessment purposes.

This study was limited to schools in which the majority of children were first and second generation British Muslims of Asian descent, so a major need was found to be English language acquisition. Some children were newly arrived immigrants from Bangladesh. Such a need will not necessarily hold true for Muslim children whose parents and perhaps grandparents were born in the UK and whose linguistic and educational needs may be very different. Situations change, therefore needs change. Furthermore, the schools in this study had been identified as those striving to respond to ethnic minority needs and were models of good practice in many instances. Elsewhere, schools might be not be as advanced in developing their response to the issues highlighted here and may well be at a different stage and level of responding to need. In short, the momentum of responding to Muslim needs should be maintained but it is essential that educationalists and policy-makers employ greater sophistication in diagnosing categories and levels of needs, and in assessing the success or failure of efforts made so far. We have to move beyond narrow and restricted definitions of needs, to respond to the differentiation which exists within the pupil population and the reality of the classroom situation. We need also to look at the broader philosophical and political concerns rising from this discussion. It is these that form the basis of the concluding chapter.

Notes

1. *Education Reform Act,* 1988, London: HMSO, ch.40.
2. As noted earlier in Chapter 4, this theory derives from the Bullock inquiry into language and holds that 'no child should be expected to cast off the mother tongue as he enters the school'. See Bullock Report, *A Language for Life,* London: HMSO.
3. Some supplementary schools for black pupils of African Caribbean descent, for example, focus on basics in education which they feel their children are failing to receive in the state school system, see for example, 'Why Discipline is the Key to Good Education', *The Voice,* Sept., 20, 1994, p.12.
4. See R. Dearing (1994) *The National Curriculum and its Assessment,* Final Report (Dearing), London: School Curriculum and Assessment Agency.
5. See for example developments in Black history and the role played by Black people in the Bible, in *The Voice,* May 17, 1994, p.10 & 21.
6. This has been evident in a recent GCSE examination in English which caused offence over subject matter, see for example, 'Subject was Offensive', *Leicester Mercury,* 16 June, 1994, p.4.

7. This is evidenced in the study I am currently conducting into Muslim girls' schooling (ESRC 1993-95), in which the majority of Muslim children aged between 5-13 are attending madrassahs after school when they might normally be doing homework.

8. Enabling legislation for parents is expressed in:
   the *Education Act,* 1981, London: HMSO, ch.60.
   the *Education (No.2) Act,* 1986, London: HMSO, ch.61.
   the *Education Reform Act* 1988, London: HMSO, ch.40 and more recently within the *Education Act* 1993, London: HMSO, ch.35.

9. See *Development of Performance Indicators: Key to Effective Management,* (1989b), London: Dept. of Education and Science.

10. See *Education (Schools) Act,* 1992, London: HMSO, ch.38.

11. See S. Wolfendale (1992) *Empowering Parents and Teachers: Working for Children,* London: Cassell.

12. On the theme of family literacy, see E. Goldsmith and R. Handel (1990) *Family Reading: An Intergenerational Approach to Literacy,* Syracuse, N.Y.: New Readers Press; and P. Hannon (1995) *Literacy, Home and School: Research and Practice in Teaching Literacy with Parents,* London: Falmer Press.

13. Concerns over the under-achievement of this group were expressed in the *Swann Report* (1985). Likewise Rattansi (1992) notes the inclusion of Mirpuri Pakistanis and raises issues over rigour in exploring the causes of underachievement. A recent study seeks to challenge a prevailing general assumption that Bangladeshi children are underachieving, see Centre for Bangladeshi Studies (1994) *Routes and Beyond: Voices from Educationally Successful Bangladeshis,* London: CBS. This study is also interesting for consideration given to teacher expectations of academic achievement among ethnic minority groups.

14. See for example G. Sarwar (1994) *British Muslims and Schools,* London: Muslim Educational Trust who argues that there should be high expectations of Muslim children and encouragement to aim for excellence; and N. Hussain (1992) 'Undereducation not Underachievement of Muslim Children in the UK', *Islamia* (1992b) 20 November, pp.6-8, who reviews statistical evidence of examination results and the implications for life chances.

Chapter 7

Conclusion

The rejection and devaluation of one's culture should not be a condition of full participation in social life (Young, 1990, p.166).

Broad philosophical concerns arise from our discussion which are relevant not only to Muslim children but to other ethnic minorities. This chapter seeks to locate the discussion in a wider context and considers i) the need to revisit multicultural education, ii) to explore the concept of cultural identity within the British context and iii) to raise implications for teacher training. In response to the issues, there follows policy recommendations to extend the debate further and so enhance educational policy for the 1990s and into the 21st century.

(i) Multiculturalism Revisited

Multicultural education became prominent in the 1970s and 1980s, as an overall attempt to respond to cultural diversity in society. The way the term has been conceptualised has depended on the goals and purpose of multicultural education and we saw, in chapter 1, that some assumed a liberal position, emphasising such issues as mutual tolerance and prejudice reduction while others advocated anti-racism aimed at radically challenging and restructuring an unjust society. Both approaches have been severely criticised for their failure to transform school experience and move beyond the rhetoric of equality. The impact of the *Education Reform Act* (ERA)[1] has done nothing to improve matters. Quite the contrary, as it is a predominantly ethnocentric, assimilationist document so the only scope for a multicultural/anti-racist dimension has laid within options, separated from the obligatory monocultural core. Rattansi (1992) summarises the situation thus:

> in a series of moves capped by the Education Reform Act the proposals for a national (or, as some were quick to point out, nation-*alist*) curriculum, the Conservative government had effectively challenged and undermined the fragile liberal consensus Swann had tried to erect in the mid-1980s (p.13).

It is this 'fragile liberal consensus' which needs to be reviewed and revitalised, as the retreat from Thatcherite ideology takes place. When the political pendulum swings, as it inevitably will, teachers will need to think through what multicultural/anti-racist education means for their schools. Lessons from the first stage of this experiment in education can be learnt while we enter a new phase made possible by the space provided as a result of the Dearing Report[2] and, increasingly, as many of the educational reforms of a Conservative Government are discarded. A slimmed down National Curriculum and a recommended calming of the system after years of upheaval should facilitate the 'revisiting' of multicultural education after the way become lost in the aftermath of assessment, standard attainment targets and the effect of local management of schools.

Developing the curriculum within the context of multicultural education requires an entire revision of teaching. Curriculum innovation involves the selection, structuring and delivery of knowledge which is balanced, accurate and appropriate; reflective of the achievement and contributions of cultural groups beyond the dominant one. For example, appropriate recognition of Islamic contributions to science and mathematics, a sensitive approach to teaching topics like the Crusades, and the promotion of positive role models, are all feasible (Dufour, 1990). Moreover,

> merely tinkering with existing ethnocentric curricula is inappropriate. All too often the curriculum is altered to include lessons on different cultural activities and is then erroneously claimed to be multicultural.

> This kind of tokenism only serves to denigrate the complexity and value of multicultural education (Squelch, 1993, p.43).

This is also the view of Banks (1989) who warns against superficial teaching practices based on the incorporation of fragmented pieces into an existing curriculum. Sadly some schools are still no further along the path of the three 'S's' of 'saris, steel bands and samosas' (Massey, 1991): indeed a few never got on that road in the first place![3] What is required now is:

> to offer students a wide variety of learning experiences and opportunities, in all subject areas and through the hidden curriculum, that will expose them to knowledge, experiences and perspectives beyond their own life-world (Squelch, p.43).

A major criticism of multicultural education, and one particularly relevant to this discussion, is the perceived promotion of Western values and the omission or disparagement of those held by minority groups. On this issue:

> parents do not wish their children to grow up in contempt for their cultural heritage and to become isolated from their own culture (ibid, p.47).

Understanding the processes of assimilation and acculturation within multicultural education is particularly pertinent:

> assimilation implies the complete and unconditional surrender of one's own culture and the adoption of the mainstream culture, resulting in the elimination of cultural differences. Acculturation, on the other hand, is a two way process whereby aspects of cultures are shared and a culture becomes modified through contact with another culture. Each culture, however, maintains its essential aspects (ibid).

At its simplest this requires learning from one another; in reality it means teachers adopting some of the perspectives of the ethnic minority pupils in the school. Perceiving curriculum from a non-Western perspective and interpreting problems in non-Western, religious terms has legitimacy and should be incorporated within an educational framework which ensures representation and contributions from a wide range of cultures.

Revisiting multicultural education also means providing a balanced curriculum, scrutinising methods of assessment, improving the school climate by challenging and not ignoring racist abuse, and developing effective home-school links. Some of the needs found in this study fall into these categories and have implications for many children besides those of Islamic background. Multicultural education should be about enhancing educational opportunity and equity for all children, away from a monocultural, ethnocentric or Britocentric focus to one which recognises and celebrates cultural diversity and most importantly, that is concerned with the high academic achievement of all pupils.

Schools need now to reassess their position along the continuum of responses to a multicultural Britain. This is not to criticise institutions which are working hard in the face of competing concerns, which in other institutions have been allowed to overwhelm development of equal educational opportunities. Revisiting should be about sharing good practice in response to the legitimate and ever-present question: what are you doing to meet the needs of the different cultural groups in your school? Revisiting multiculturalism requires learning from the mistakes of the 1980s; defining very carefully the purpose, justification and implementation of policy. Since the Burnage tragedy (1989) paralysis has set in, with many schools finding the pressures of the National Curriculum a convenient, yet very real excuse to avoid the issues.

Meanwhile, racism, both institutional and individual, continues, frequently in the form of abuse and bullying[4]. Schools have to move on:

> Positive images in the textbooks and classrooms are neutralised if institutional practices elsewhere in the school or college are racist. Whole-school policies are therefore essential (Dufour, 1990, p.128)

Furthermore, some schools may misrepresent abusive situations:

> many attacks against Muslims are recorded as 'racist' when, in fact, they have been targeted because they are Muslim (Sarwar, 1994, p.27)

Do non-Muslim teachers fully understand the difference between religious and racial bigotry? Both need to be understood by teachers and both should now be considered within policy on discrimination:

> because of their distinctive dress, Muslims are easy targets, particularly Muslim girls who chose to wear hijab (head covering) (ibid)[5].

Pupils of other faith groups such as Sikh, Hindu, Jewish, Brethren or Rastafarian, can also be subject to abuse due to their appearance. Some children might in fact suffer double-edged prejudice and discrimination evoked by both their ethnicity and their religion. The issue has to be seen within a broad context of promoting social justice for all children[6]. What is required is a rethinking of educational interventions and strategies, if racism and cultural difference are to be adequately addressed in the 1990s and beyond.

(ii) Cultural Identity

Issues of identity strike at the heart of parental concern over multiculturalism. Increasingly, there is a recognition of the enormous differentiation and diversity in the historical and cultural experiences of minorities which Hall (1992) descibes as 'the new ethnicities', displacing previously stable political categories. As discussed in chapter 1, this new cultural politics engages with rather than suppresses difference and represents a broader concept of ethnicity, challenging a restricted concept of what it is to be British. 'We are all in a sense, *ethnically* located and our ethnic identities are crucial to our subjective sense of who we are' (ibid, p.258). The importance of identity is echoed in the writings of Islamic theorists (Sarwar, 1983; Ashraf, 1985; Yaseen 1992; Raza, 1993), and is an issue of which schools should take account. Debate over what it means to be 'British' features as an important element within multicultural education. Realistically, assimilation is unlikely to be feasible or acceptable, since:

> it is unreasonable to expect us to assimilate and lose our identity, for a community with such a strong religious identity total assimilation is absurdity (Sarwar, 1994, p.30)

Similarly,

> the expectation that the Afro-Caribbean and Asian minorities would simply blend into a homogeneous British or even English stew, perhaps adding some harmless spice, was revealed as not only hopelessly unrealistic but symptomatic of a form of racism which regarded 'Britishness' and 'Westernness' as the only touchstones of cultural value (Rattansi, 1992, p.13).

The Swann Report stopped at the West Indian and Asian divide and never fully explored the huge varieties of difference within these categories. 'Sub-ethnicities' have not been adequately explored, argues Rattansi, and consequently any discussion of needs has generally been subsumed under generic label such as 'Asian', for example, which does not adequately describe children of vast cultural differences and identities. This study has pointed to the importance of deconstructing the term 'Muslim' in such a way as to recognise the huge differentiation within the category and to provide more refinement and determination of what needs require accommodation, for which pupils, at what level and for what reasons. In addition, as this study shows, cultural-religious needs may be relevant for many Muslim children but questions concerning language acquisition, for example, may be more restricted to children of newly arrived families. It is a mistake to label all Muslims of Asian descent as in need of English improvement — this is patently obvious from the success in this country of generations of Muslim children of Indian and Pakistani origin. Furthermore:

> a range of 'black' groups have begun to explore, construct and express identities and experiences not exhausted by the experience of and struggle against racism, or the polarisation between social democratic and revolutionary strategic positions ... there is emerging a new cultural politics of difference which overlays the older ethnic differences ... Neither the multiculturalist nor the anti-racist movement in education has yet engaged with these 'new ethnicities' (ibid, p.41).

Along similar lines, Young (1990) rejects an assimilationist model and states that:

> the politics [of difference] asserts that ... groups have distinct culture, experiences, and perceptions on social life with humanly positive meaning, some of which may even be superior to the culture and perspectives of mainstream society (p.166).

The over-simplifications previously informing educational policy and practice in the field of race and education needs to be challenged. People build their own social identity and this may clash with those of the indigenous population. How, then, does society preserve ethnic boundaries, and the distinction, if one can be drawn, as to whether the identity is ethnic or religious? This is highly apposite in the case of Muslims, for they need to 'fit in without being swallowed up' by a Western society[7] which they see as being buttressed by the school system; undermining social identity and failing to recognise and respond to religous/cultural needs (Sarwar, 1994). So there is a fear that the more a Muslim becomes integrated, the less 'Muslim' they will be. To prevent loss of identity concerted efforts are made by Muslim communities to provide supplementary education, as outlined in chapter 3, and to express concerns and demands to local and national government.

The question then becomes: what is being British within an Islamic construction? Being a British Muslim is a matter of negotiation between two cultures, yet, as one pupil at a school in the study told the author in informal discussion, 'we're always Asian, never British!'. This epitomises the difficulty British society has in coming to terms with religious and national identity. Clearly, children may wish to be Muslim *and* British, and indeed proud to be both. Notions of identity are always changing and the fact must be accepted that children may have a dual or multiple realities. The pathology-deficit model, discussed earlier in chapter 1, in which ethnic minorities such as Muslims are perceived as the problem, still exists but must yield to looking at structures which are sufficiently flexible and which prevent the marginalisation of children. A British-Muslim identity should be nurtured in response to the shifting notions of cultural identity.

Developments in Europe demonstrate the increasing politicisation of Muslim communities, and the need to differentiate between what it means to be a Muslim, the variety of Muslim communities and the variety of Muslim needs (Lahnemann et al, 1983; Anwar, 1984; Etienne, 1990; Vertovec, 1995). It is difficult to acquire accurate and up-to-date information about the nature of Muslim communities to which schools are attached, but ignorance is a poor excuse for educationalists. One Muslim headteacher in the study remarked:

> since you came in contact with us ... you see our children, when you see us here we are not people with two horns, frightening people or, how do you say, fundamentalists — not that word as they use it ... We are ordinary people trying to live by our faith sincerely, as best as possible and our faith has lots of responsibilities for us ... but we are trying our best.

The problems experienced by Muslim parents and children are in many cases shared by other ethnic or religious groups in state schools. Children leave their familiar environment to study in a new social, linguistic and cultural environment away from their family. Acquiring the cultural values of the school and the indigenous community is seen as part of that experience. Yet education is not about accepting the status quo: minority groups can demand changes and the accommodation of their needs. It requires schools to be responsive to these needs: to consider the extent to which they can and should respond to cultural diversity in the classroom. It calls for effective home-school relations, as discussed in the previous chapter, to provide adequate and creative channels of communication, and for parents to be well-informed of the educational philosophy which shapes their children's future.

Muslims, like other groups, are seen as using religion and linguistics as shields against cultural loss and identity. One Muslim administrator in the study maintained that some element of assimilation is bound to take place and is pending, however disquieting to older generations, but whilst acculturation and assimilation continue, it is the manner in which this is accomplished which needs consideration.

(iii) Teacher Training

The issues raised so far clearly point to the need to consider the adequacy of teacher training with regard to cultural diversity in British society. Teachers cannot be expected to translate educational theory into practice without adequate training, both pre-service and in-service, in multicultural skills, knowledge and values. Within the last decade, how much progress has been made in requiring that a multicultural/anti-racist dimension permeates teaching and that there is regular input in initial courses and regular inservice for practising teachers? The Rampton (1981) and Swann (1985) Reports highlighted the importance of in-service education of teachers, and the Council for the Accreditation of Teacher Education required that intending teachers be introduced to issues concerning the ethnic composition of Britain (Pumphrey and Verma, 1990), but the momentum has now stopped. Muslims are Britain's largest minority group: yet 'educating Muslim children', is no part of teacher training programmes or only within a diluted notion of multicultural education. Is space allowed for programmes addressing religious background, Islamic philosophies and diversity within Muslim communities? There is a danger that, as in the classroom, multicultural/anti-racist teaching is giving way in teacher training institutions to issues such as assessment and attainment targets. Furthermore, what component of teacher training programmes examines the critical importance of home-school links, let alone the inclusion of ethnic minority parents? Yet the reality for most societies today is that:

> teachers are required to work not only with culturally diverse groups of pupils but also with parents from diverse cultural and socio-economomic backgrounds. It is essential for teachers to be able to co-operate and communicate with these parents and to involve all parents, including semi-literate and low income parents, in school and home-based activities (Squelch, p.46).

A further issue is the selection and recruitment of teachers from minority backgrounds, raised briefly in chapter 4. Despite moves to establish private Muslim schools, the majority of Muslim children are likely to remain in the state system due to a variety of factors, including availability of funding and parental preference. There are already insufficient teachers of ethnic minority background in the state system, and fewer still who practise Islam. Coupled with this is the marginalisation of many black teaching staff because they are employed in Section 11 posts or community language teams (Rattansi, 1992). Initiatives to increase the number of teachers from ethnic minority backgrounds have been ineffectual thus far (Sarwar, 1994), and the very existence of 'Section 11' funding is under threat[8]. Accordingly, non-Muslim staff will increasingly need to have an understanding and awareness of the needs of Muslim children.

Innovative and creative ways need to be developed to help state school teachers, almost all non-Muslims, become better informed. Non-Muslim headteachers in this study disclosed a genuine desire for much-needed access to knowledge of Islam for themselves and their staff. A possible strategy would be for them to have access to a Muslim school. Twinning of schools takes place internationally and between urban and rural schools in the UK. This study shows that there are Muslim schools established around London, Bradford, Leicester and Bolton, for example, and in the same locality are state schools with high numbers of Muslim children. The profound changes in funding of schools means that distinctions between schools are becoming somewhat blurred, allowing bridges to be built. By an appropriate twinning arrangement, state school teachers could be provided with access to an Islamic environment where they could gain first hand information about Islamic values and Islamic perspectives within the curriculum. Reciprocally, teachers in Muslim schools could access material and human resources which would benefit their work and enhance professional development.

Any initiative in twinning should be seen in terms of denominational as well as ethnic factors. Exchanges between a denominational and non-denominational school could lead to cultural projects and sporting events, bringing individuals and groups together on a non-sectarian basis. Or teachers could be seconded between schools for short periods. Ethos is imbibed through teachers and not just through the curriculum, and such exchanges would enable the sharing of invaluable knowledge and cultural awareness. Twinning between schools during the celebrations of religious festivals could also involve pupils and enhance their knowledge of different faith groups.

Finally, within this theme of teacher education is the issue of assessment. Cultural awareness and assessment go hand in hand: without a rigorous understanding of cultural background, attitudes and values, how can assessment claim to be remotely free of cultural bias? Education should be about building on successes rather than highlighting failure — which is what the current narrow form of assessment is likely to achieve. Cultural, religious and linguistic variations have to be taken into account in testing, and second or third language acquisition should not act as a barrier to achievement and progression. Positive responses to issues of assessment and equity, the twinning of schools, recruitment of ethnic minority staff and cultural awareness could assist teachers in their task of meeting the needs of Muslim pupils and other children in schools.

(iv) Policy Agenda

From the earlier discussion in chapter 5 of needs relating to English language acquisition, a balanced curriculum and effective home-school links, the focus shifted in chapter 6 to broadening and redefining the concept of needs. These concerns raised some philosophical and political issues about multiculturalism, cultural identity and teacher training, which were discussed in the present chapter and pointed clearly to the need for policy recommendations for future planning. The characteristics of the next phase of needs which schools have to face are that they are:

- heavily resource led;

- require a high level of commitment and energy from head-teacher and staff; and

- strike at the very core of the National Curriculum, which is centrally driven.

Local education authorities' approach to multiculturalism and equal opportunities took many forms in the 1980s and this is likely to hold true for initiatives in the 1990s and beyond. However, attention will also have to be given by central government to improving aspects of social justice. Implications for specific policy formation centre on:

- *English language support* whereby Section 11 funding is protected, new models of provision are explored and the generational issues of language needs are incorporated into policy initiatives with adequate levels of finance;

- *Multiculturalism* in which recognition is given to the fact that all children, regardless of their background, are capable of experiencing a sense of powerlessness. Attention must be given to differentiation within cultural groups and the need to expand existing concepts of discrimination to include matters of religion as well as race, social class and gender;

- *The role of parents* whereby family strengths rather than deficits are highlighted, and there is recognition of the curriculum of the home and encouragement of parental work in facilitating learning in partnership with the school;

- *Teacher training* in which input on cultural diversity is improved in both initial and in-service training, with implications for effecting better relationships within the pupil-parent-school triangle; and, finally,

- *More research* in which vigorous government funding into cultural pluralism and its implications for schools is no longer conspicuous by its absence. The call for more inquiry may seem trite but in the post-Swann/post-ERA era, the issue

135

remains as vital as ever, especially in light of the marginalisation of equal opportunities of late. When located in a
broader context, issues of language and cultural identity have
implications for many groups in this country. Equal opportunity rhetoric by itself has no substance or meaning: the
theory needs to be translated into practice.

So far a balancing act of accommodation in British schools has delivered
a pragmatic yet fragmentary approach to responding to the educational
needs of Muslim children. Some Muslim parents have perceived efforts
thus far as inadequate and have instead turned to private Muslim schools
which have been established in the last decade. Unless questions arising
from categories two and three of the theoretical framework outlined in
chapter 4 and expanded in chapter 5, are addressed with some urgency,
this balancing act will become more and more precarious and the demands
for separate, government financed support for these schools will increase
significantly. The Swann Report (1985) warned that if Muslim needs were
not accommodated within the state school system, parents would be fully
justified in choosing Muslim schools. The fact must be recognised that
Muslim schools, however undesirable because the children are kept
separate, will prevail with or without public funding, since it is impossible
to satisfy the expressed needs of *all* Muslim parents. As suggested in
earlier chapters, it is more helpful to ask: to what extent can and should
the common school respond to cultural diversity? An appropriate Islamic
dimension or perspective within the common curriculum is advocated but
the curriculum cannot be totally Islamised. However, it is possible to fund
separate institutions where it can be, such as the schools already operating
in the independent sector.

Recent legislation may ensure that finance is forthcoming and parental
choice, as espoused in Education Acts of the 1980s and in European and
international conventions to which Britain is a party[9], is translated into
reality. There are now compelling political reasons for giving public
funding to qualifying Muslim schools, and a percentage of existing
institutions (approximately 25) might benefit. But if the number of such
schools increases, who will staff them and what will be their qualifications? Furthermore, and most pertinent to this discussion, what of the
approximately 95% of Muslim children who will probably remain in the
state school system? Clearly, they will require teachers who have an

understanding and sensitivity to their needs and a general commitment to developing policy which moves away from the restrictive strait-jacket of the National Curriculum towards incorporating space for appropriate curriculum development and assessment as identified in this book. Finally, simply tinkering with the system or providing insufficient financial support will leave the concept of equal opportunities exactly where it is now for many children: a paper exercise containing pious but empty rhetoric.

In the aftermath of *The Satanic Verses*, debate was generated in Britain about the social and educational needs of Muslims. Media treatment of the Rushdie affair, the Gulf War and the Bosnian crisis, which often presents negative Muslim images, has added to a climate of 'Islamaphobia'. It is necessary to view the place of Muslims in Britain, without implying a threat to the indigenous population. Accommodation is required, not confrontation, to find the equilibrium between majority and minority needs to avoid the marginalisation of ethnic minority group children. To find this balance will require compromise on all sides. Ethnic minorities will have to relinquish some of the their cultural heritage. For their part, teachers seeking to meet the educational needs of children from a diversity of backgrounds will have to ensure that multicultural antiracist strategies remain at the forefront of their practice. Society as a whole needs to move away from a utopian ideal of total assimilation towards a more pragmatic realism[10] in which we celebrate a cultural pluralism. Until this is recognised by adults, children will have to struggle on alone to negotiate an acceptable position in the home and at school. If, however, society does make such a move, children of Islam and from other ethnic minority groups will at last have the parity of esteem that is essential in the formulation of their status and identity in British society.

Notes

1. *Education Reform Act* 1988, London: HMSO, ch.40.
2. See R. Dearing (1994) *The National Curriculum and its Assessment,* Final Report (Dearing), London: Schools Curriculum and Assessment Agency.
3. See S. Tomlinson (1990) *Multicultural Education in White Schools,* London: B. T. Batsford Ltd.
4. See for example, D. Gillborn (1995) *Racism and Antiracism in Real Schools,* Buckingham: Open University Press; 'Race Attack and Race Card', *Asian Times,* 11 June 1994, p.4; 'Fascist Thug Guilty of Mob Savagery', *The Voice,* June 14, 1994, p.5; 'A Charter for Race Equality', *The Voice,* June 14, 1994 p.7; and 'Court Winks at BNP Thuggery', *Asian Times,* 25 June, 1994, p.4. This theme of racism also concerns the issue of exclusion and ethnicity with claims that young black boys are four times more likely to be excluded from school than their white peers, see for example, the Institute of Race Relations (1994) *Outcast England: How Schools Exclude Black Children,* London: IRR; C. Wright (1992) *Race Relations in the Primary School,* London: David Fulton Publishers; and 'School Exclusion Scandal Continues', *The Voice,* June 14, 1994, p.12.
5. This view has been confirmed by some of the girls interviewed in my present research of Muslim schools, as a general area of concern.
6. For more on this theme see R. Connel (1993) *Schools and Social Justice,* Philadelphia: Temple University Press; and L. Burton and G. Weiner (1990) 'Social Justice and the National Curriculum', *Research Papers in Education* 5(3), pp.193-207.
7. The expression 'how to fit in without being swallowed up!' is attributed to my doctoral student Roger Ali, Cambridgeshire Youth Service, who is exploring this issue for his forthcoming dissertation, School of Education, University of Nottingham.
8. For more on the issue of Section 11 funding see 'Section 11 Cuts', *British Muslims Monthly Survey,* 1994 2(8), p.19.
9. See R. Beddard (1980) *Human Rights and Europe,* 2nd ed., London: Sweet and Maxwell; F. G. Jacobs (1975) *The European Convention on Human Rights,* Oxford: Clarendon Press; and A. H. Robertson (1982) *Human Rights in the World,* 2nd ed., Manchester: Manchester University Press, for discussion of Britain's undertakings via the European Convention on Human Rights and for international human rights declarations to which Britain is a signatory.
10. This theme is discussed in depth in H. T. Trueba (1989) *Raising Silent Voices,* New York: Harper-Collins Publishers Inc.

Bibliography

Akhtar, S. (1993) *The Muslim Parents' Handbook*, London: Ta-Ha Publishing.

Alavi, K. (1989) *Role of the Mosque in the Muslim Community*, Birmingham: Birmingham Central Mosque.

Al-Faruqi, I. R. (1982) *Islamisation of Knowledge: General Principles and Workplan*, Hendon: International Institution of Islamic Thought.

Anwar, M. (1982) *Young Muslims in a Multicultural Society: their needs and policy implications*, Leicester: The Islamia Foundation.

Anwar, M. (1984) *Social and Cultural Perspectives on Muslims in Western Europe*, Birmingham: CSIC.

Anwar, M. (1993) *Muslims in Britain: the 1991 Census and Other Statistical Sources*, Birmingham: Centre for the Study of Christian and Muslim Relations, Paper 9.

Armytage, W. H. G. (1964) *Four Hundred Years of English Education*, London: Cambridge University Press.

Ashraf, S. A. (1985) *New Horizons in Muslim Education*, London: Hodder and Stoughton.

Ashraf, S. A. (1986) Foreword to Halstead, J. M. (1986) *The Case for Muslim Voluntary-Aided Schools: Some Philosophical Reflections*, Cambridge: The Islamic Agency.

Ashraf, S. A. (1988) editorial in *Muslim Educational Quarterly* 5(3), pp.1-7.

Ashraf, S. A. (1993) 'The Role of Muslim Youth in a Multi- Religious Society', *Muslim Education Quarterly*, 11(1), p.3-13.

Ashraf, S. A. (1994) 'Faith-Based Education: A Theoretical Shift from the Secular to the Transcendent', *Muslim Education Quarterly*, 11(2), pp.3-8.

Asian Times (1993) 'Islamia School Loses Fight for Voluntary Aided Status', August 24, p.1.

Asian Times (1994) 'Race Attack and Race Card', 11 June, p.4.

Asian Times (1994) 'Court Winks at BNP Thuggery', 25 June, p.4.

Association of Muslim Schools (1990) *Islamic Studies Guide*, Transvaal: South African Institute for Islamic Educational Research.

Ba-Janus, I. (1988) 'Future Directions in Islamisation of Knowledge', *The American Journal of Islamic Social Sciences*, 5(1), pp.13-28.

Banks, J. A. (1989) *Multicultural Education: Issues and Perspectives*, London: Allyn and Bacon.

Banks, J. A. and Lynch, J. (eds) (1986) *Multicultural Education in Western Societies*, London: Holt, Rinehart and Winston.

Barrell, G. and Partington, J. (1985) 6th ed. *Teachers and the Law*, London: Methuen.

Beddard, R. (1980) *Human Rights and Europe*, 2nd ed., London: Sweet and Maxwell.

Belford, L. (1965) *Introduction to Judaism*, London: Darton, Longman and Todd.

Berliner, W. (1993) 'Muslims Stand Their Ground', *Education Guardian*, 23 March, pp.6-7.

Bone, A. (1983) *Girls and Girls-Only Schools: A Review of the Evidence*, London: Equal Opportunities Commission.

Bullock Report (1975) *A Language for Life*, London: HMSO.

Burnage Report (1989) *Murder in the Playground*, London: Longsight Press.

Brah, A. (1992) 'Difference, Diversity and Differentiation', in J. Donald and A. Rattansi, *Race, Culture and Difference*, London: Sage Publications.

Brock, C. and Tulasiewicz, W. (1985) (eds), *Cultural Identity and Educational Policy*, London: Croom Helm.

British Muslims' Monthly Survey, (1993) 'Changes in School Uniform, Derbyshire', 1(4), p.10.

British Muslims' Monthly Survey, (1993) 'Muslim Pupil Wins a Place in a Girls' School', 1(9), p.10.

British Muslims' Monthly Survey, (1993a) 'Statistics — Muslim Population of Britain: A Short Report' 1(10), pp.4-5.

British Muslims' Monthly Survey, (1993) 'Islamia School, Brent', 1(10), p.15.

British Muslims' Monthly Survey, (1993) 'School Uniform Problems', 1(10), p.16.

British Muslims' Monthly Survey, (1994) 'School Uniform Problems Crawley', 1(10), p.16.

British Muslims' Monthly Survey, (1994) 'Prayer Room For One', 2(2), p.12.

British Muslims' Monthly Survey, (1994) 'Religions Unite Against Secularism', 2(2), p.13.

British Muslims' Monthly Survey, (1994) 'Drive for More Teachers', 2(3), p.20.

British Muslims' Monthly Survey, (1994) 'Boys' Boarding School Proposed, Sheffield', 2(3), p.23.

British Muslims' Monthly Survey, (1994) 'Provision of Halal Meat', 2(4), pp.3-4.

British Muslims' Monthly Survey, (1994) 'New Syllabus for GCSE Islam', 2(4), p.20.

British Muslims' Monthly Survey, (1994) 'Mixed Dance Classes', 2(4), p.22.

British Muslims' Monthly Survey, (1994) 'Developments on Halal Meat Control', 2(5), p.3.

British Muslims' Monthly Survey, (1994) 'Muslim Boys School, Leicester', 2(5), p.18.

British Muslims' Monthly Survey, (1994) 'Muslim Girls and School Uniform', 2(5), p.18.

British Muslims' Monthly Survey, (1994) 'Bristol Single-Sex Schools to Close', 2(5), p.19.

British Muslims' Monthly Survey, (1994) 'Reports on Bangladeshi Writer', 2(6), p.3.

British Muslims' Monthly Survey, (1994) 'Bradford Muslim Girls' School', 2(6), pp.20-21, and 1(10), p.15.

British Muslims' Monthly Survey, (1994) 'Asian Governors' Forum', 2(7), p.31.

British Muslims' Monthly Survey, (1994) 'Section 11 Funding', 2(7), p.31.

British Muslims' Monthly Survey, (1994) 'Women Convert to Islam', 2(8), p.17.

British Muslims' Monthly Survey (1994) 'Section 11 Cuts', 2(8), p.19.

British Muslims' Monthly Survey, (1994) 'Islamia and VA Status', 2(8), p.20).

Brock, C. and Tulasiewicz, W. (1985) (eds) *Cultural Identity and Educational Policy*, London: Croom Helm.

Burton, L. and Weiner, G. (1990) 'Social Justice and the National Curriculum', Research Papers in Education, 5(3), pp.193-207.

Carroll, B. and Hollinshead, G. (1993) 'Ethnicity and Conflict in Physical Education', British Educational Research Journal, 19(1), pp.59-76.

Castles, S. (1984) Here for Good, London: Pluto.

Centre for the Study of Islam and Christian-Muslim Relations (1985) Report of seminar held at Westhill College, Selly Oak, Birmingham. Citizenship and religious education: Multifaith and denominational schools.

Centre for Bangladeshi Studies (1994) Routes and Beyond: Voices from Educationally Successful Bangladeshis, London: CBS.

Children's Legal Centre (1994) 'Sex Education', Childright, 105, April, p.7.

Choudhury, M. A. (1993) 'A Critical Examination of the Concept of Islamization of Knowledge in Contemporary Times', Muslim Education Quarterly, 10(4), pp.3-34.

Commission for Racial Equality (1990) Schools of Faith, Elliot House, 10-12 Allington Street, London SW1E 5EH.

Connel, R. (1993) Schools and Social Justice, Philadelphia: Temple University Press.

Corner, T. (1988) Equality for Educational Opportunity for Pupils from Ethnic Minority Families, paper for European Parents' Association Conference, Strasbourg.

Craft, A. and Bardell, G. (eds) (1984) Curriculum Opportunities in a Multicultural Society, London: Harper Educational.

Cumper, D. (1990) 'Muslim Schools: Implications of the Education Reform Act 1988', New Community, 16(3), pp.379-389.

Curtis, S. J. and Boultwood, M. E. (1966) Introducing History of English Education since 1800, 4th ed., London: University Tutorial Press.

Dabene, C. L. (1993) 'Some Aspects of Multilingualism and their Educational Implications', Language, Culture and the Curriculum, special issue 'Towards Global Multi-lingualism', 6(3), pp.241- 248.

Daniel, N. W. (1968) Racial Discrimination in England, Harmondsworth: Penguin.

Darsh, S. M. and Lemu, B. A. (1992) The Mosque and Muslim Women, Port-Louis, Mauritius: Qur'an House and the Council of Muslim Women.

Dearing, R. (1994) The National Curriculum and its Assessment, Final Report (Dearing), London: School Curriculum and Assessment Agency.

Deem, R. (1984) *Co-education Reconsidered,* Milton Keynes: Open University Press.

Department for Education (1991) *The Parent's Charter. You and Your Child's Education,* London: HMSO.

Department for Education (1994) *Circular on Religious Education and Collective Worship,* Circular 1/94, London: DFE.

Department of Education and Science, (1965) *The Education of Immigrants,* Circular 7/65, London: DES.

Department of Education and Science (1977) *Education in Schools: A Consultative Document* (Green Paper, Cmnd 6869), London: HMSO.

Department of Education and Science (1989a) *The Education Reform Act 1988: Religious Education and Collective Worship,* Circular No. 3/89, London: HMSO.

Department of Education and Science (1989b) *Development of Performance Indicators: Key to Effective Management,* London: DES.

Department of Education and Science (1992) *Art in the National Curriculum,* London: HMSO.

Department of Education and Science (1992) *Music in the National Curriculum,* London: HMSO.

Department of Education and Science (1992) *Non-Statutory Guidance, Art,* London: HMSO.

Department of Education and Science (1992) *Physical Education in the National Curriculum,* London: HMSO.

Donald, J. and Rattansi, A. (1992) *Race, Culture and Difference,* London: Sage Publications.

Dufour, B. (1990) *A New Social Curriculum: A Guide to Cross-Curricular Issues,* Cambridge: Cambridge University Press.

Durham, M. (1989) 'The Religious Issue that Won't Go Away', *The Guardian,* March 14, p.12.

Eggleston, J. (1990) 'Can anti-racist teaching survive the 1988 Education Act', *Multicultural Teaching,* 8(3), pp.9-11.

Ellis, R. (1985) *Understanding Second Language Acquisition,* Oxford: Oxford University Press.

Etienne, B. (1990) *L'Islam en France,* Paris: Editions du Centre National de la Recherche Scientifique, 15, quai Anatole France, 75700.

Falaturi, A. and Tworuschka, U. (1991) *A Guide to the Presentation of Islam in School Textbooks,* Birmingham: Centre for the Study of Islam and Christian-Muslim Relations, Paper No.8.

Follain, M. (1989) 'Political Storm Breaks over Muslim Scarves', *Times Educational Supplement,* 3 November, p.17.

Francis, J. (1994) 'The Age of Safer Sex', *Community Care*, January, pp.18-19.

Gilborn, D. (1995) (pending) *Racism and Antiracism in Real Schools*, Buckingham: Open University Press.

Goldsmith, E. and Handel, R. (1990) *Family Reading: An Intergenerational Approach to Literacy*, Syracuse, N.Y.: New Readers Press.

The Guardian (1994a) 'Covered in Confusion', October 6, pp.10-11.

The Guardian (1994b) 'Jewish Identity Crisis Fuelled by Out-of-date Leaders of the Faith', June 7, p.5.

Hall, S. (1992) 'New Ethnicities', in J. Donald and A. Rattansi, *Culture and Difference*, London: Sage Publications.

Halliday, F. (1994) 'The Literal versus the Liberal', *Times Higher Educational Supplement*, August 5, p.19.

Halstead, M. (1986) *The Case for Muslim Voluntary-Aided Schools Some Philosophical Reflections,* Cambridge: The Islamic Academy.

Halstead, M. (1988) *Education, Justice and Cultural Diversity: An Examination of the Honeyford Affair 1984-5,* London: Falmer Press.

Haneef, S. (1979) *What Everyone Should Know About Islam and Muslims,* Lahore: Kazi Publications.

Hannon, P. (1995) (pending) *Literacy, Home and School: Research and Practice in Teaching Literacy with Parents,* London: Falmer Press.

Hermansen, M. K. (1991) 'Two-Way Acculturation: Muslim Women in America between Individual Choice (Liminality) and Community Affiliation (Communitas)' in *The Muslims of America*, Y. Y. Hadda, Oxford: Oxford University Press.

Hiro, D. (1973) *Black British, White British,* Harmondsworth: Penguin Books.

Hodge, H. (1899) 'The Problem Teacher', *Fortnightly Review*, 65, pp.853-862.

Hulmes, E. (1989) *Education and Cultural Diversity*, London: Longman.

Husain, S. S. and Ashraf, S. A. (1979) *Crisis in Muslim Education*, Sevenoaks: Hodder and Stoughton.

Hussain, F. (1984) *Muslim Women*, New York: St. Martin's Press.

Hussain, M. (1990) Personal correspondence, 27 November 1990, Headteacher, Madrassa Karima, Supplementary School, 14 Berridge Road, Nottingham NG7 6HR.

Hussain, N. (1992) 'Undereducation not Underachievement of Muslim Children in the UK', *Islamia*, 20, November, pp.6-8.

Hyman, A. (1985) *Muslim Fundamentalism*, London: The Institute for the Study of Culture.

Idris, J. S. (1987) 'The Islamisation of the Sciences: Its Philosophy and Methodology', *The American Journal of Islamic Social Sciences*, 4(2), pp.201-208.

Iqra Trust (1991a) *Meeting the Needs of Muslim Pupils*, London: Iqra Trust.

Iqra Trust (1991b) *Participating in School Governing Bodies*, London: Iqra Trust.

The Independent (1994) 'Sex Lesson Guidelines Condemned', June 15, p.2.

Institute of Race Relations (1994) *Outcast England: How Schools Exclude Black Children*, London: IRR.

Islamia: National Muslim Education Newsletter (1992a) 'Education (Schools) Bill Amendments', (18), April, p.2, London: Islamia.

Islamia: National Muslim Education Newsletter (1992b) 'Under-education not Underachievement of Muslim Children in the UK', (20), November, pp.6-8.

Islamia: National Muslim Education Newsletter (1994) 'A Muslim Boys Secondary School', (23), March, pp.6-7.

Islamic Educational Trust (1991) *Muslims in Britain: A Statistical Survey*, Education and Training Unit, No.8, Course 30/31, January 1991.

Islamic Foundation and Training Unit (1991) *Muslims in Britain*, London: IFTU.

Jacobs, F. G. (1975) *The European Convention on Human Rights*, Oxford: Clarendon Press.

Jeffcoate, R. (1981) 'Why Multicultural Education', *Education 3-13*, 9(1), pp.4-7.

Joly, D. (1989) Muslims in Europe. Ethnic minorities and education in Britain: interaction between the Muslim community and Birmingham schools in, Research Papers No.41. Centre for the Study of Islam and Christian-Muslim Relations, Selly Oak Colleges, Birmingham.

Jones, G., Bastiani, J., Bell, G. and Chapman, C. (1992) *A Willing Partnership* (final report), London: Royal Society of Arts.

Jowell, B. et al (1989) *British Social Attitudes*, Aldershot: Gower Publishing Company.

Karim, I. (1976) *Muslim Children in British Schools: Their Rights and Duties,* Birmingham: The Straight Path.

Kazamias, K. (1966) *Education and the Quest for Modernity in Turkey,* London: Allen and Unwin.

Kodamongbe, M. N. (1965) *Education in Turkey,* Istanbul: Ministry of Education.

Labour Party (1989) *Multicultural Education: Labour's Policy for Schools,* The Labour Party: 150 Walworth Road, London SE17 1JT.

Lahnemann, J., Neilsen and Razvi, M. (1983) *Muslim Children in Europe's Schools,* Birmingham: Centre for the Study of Islam and Christian-Muslim Relations.

Lawton, D. (1980) *The Politics of the School Curriculum,* London: Routledge and Kegan Paul.

Leicester, M. C. (1989) *Multicultural Education from Theory to Practice,* Windsor: NFER: Nelson.

Leicester Mercury (1994) 'Subject was Offensive', 16 June, p.4.

Liell, P. and Saunders, J. B. (1984) *The Law of Education,* London: Butterworth.

Lightbown, P. and Spada, N. (1993) *How Languages are Learned,* Oxford: Oxford University Press.

Lodge, M. (1990) 'A Rearguard Action by the Soldiers of Christ', *Times Educational Supplement,* 2 November, pp.12-13.

Lustig, R. (1990) 'Faith Schools Hope for More Charity', *The Independent,* March 17, p.5.

Lynch, J. (1988) *Prejudice Reduction and Schools,* London: Cassell.

Mabud, S. A. (1992) 'A Muslim Response to the Education Reform Act of 1988', *British Journal of Religious Education* (14), pp.88-98.

Macbeth, A. (1989) *Involving Parents: Effective Parent-Teacher Relations,* Oxford: Heinemann Educational Books Ltd.

MacCleod, F. (1985) *Parents in Partnership: Involving Muslim Parents in their Children's Education,* London: Community Education Development Centre.

Marland, M. (1983) *Parenting, Schooling and Mutual Learning,* advance paper for the EEC School and Family Conference, Luxembourg. Also published in J. Bastiani (ed) (1988) *Parents and Teachers 2: From Policy to Practice,* London: NFER-Nelson.

Massey, I. (1991) *More Than Skin Deep,* London: Hodder and Stoughton.

McCrystal, M. (1990) 'Is Rushdie the Beginning?' *The Sunday Times*, 28 May, pp.22-29.

McDermot, M. Y. and Ashan, M. M. (1980) *The Muslim Guide*, London: The Islamic Foundation.

McGee, P. (1992) *Teaching Transcultural Care*, London: Chapman and Hall.

McLaughlin, B. (1987) *Theories of Second-Language Acquisition*, London: Edward Arnold (Publishers) Ltd.

McLean, M. (1985) 'Private Supplementary Schools and the Ethnic Challenge to State Education in Britain', in C. Brock and W. Tulasiewicz (eds) *Cultural Identity and Educational Policy*, London: Croom Helm.

McMahon, A. and Wallace, M. (1993) 'Developmental Planning: Surprise Outcomes for Multiracial Primary Schools', *Management in Education*, 7(1), pp.14-15.

Midgeley, S. (1989) 'Muslims turn to separate schools to preserve Islamic faith', *The Independent*, 20 January, p.9.

Milner, D. (1983) *Children and Race Ten Years On*, London: Ward Lock.

Modood, T. (1992) 'British Asian Muslims and the Rushdie Affair' in J. Donald and A. Rattansi (eds) *Race, Culture and Difference*, London: Sage Publications.

Mullard, C. (1981) *Racism, Society and Schools*, London: University of London.

Muslim Educational Trust (1992) 'Comments on the Government White Paper: Choice and Diversity', London: MET.

National Curriculum Council (1989) *Consultative Report on Technology*, London: Department of Education and Science.

National Curriculum Council (1992) *Non-Statutory Guidance, Music*, York: NCC.

National Curriculum Council (1992) *Non-Statutory Guidance, Physical Education*, York: NCC.

National Union of Teachers (1984) *Religious Education in a Multi-Faith Society: A Discussion Paper*. London: NUT.

Nielsen, J. S. (1981) 'Muslim Education at Home and Abroad', *British Journal of Religious Education*, Spring, pp.94-99 and p.107.

Nielson, J. S. (1986) A survey of British local authority response to Muslim needs, in *Research Papers: Muslims in Europe*. No.30/31. Centre for the Study of Islam and Christian-Muslim Relations, Selly Oak Colleges, Birmingham B29 6LE.

Nielson, J. (1987) Introduction to Islam and religious education in England, in *Europe-Research Papers* No.3, Centre for the Study of Islam and Christian-Muslim Relations, Selly Oak Colleges, Birmingham B29 6LE.

Packer, J. I. (1958) *Fundamentalism and the Word of God*, London: Inter-Varsity Fellowship.

Palmer, D. (1990) 'Culture and Education: an investigation of issues arising from the demand for separate schools for Muslim children', Unpublished M.Ed. dissertation, University of Nottingham.

Parker-Jenkins, M. (1991) 'Muslim Matters: An Exploration of the Needs of Muslim Children', *New Community*, 17(4), pp.569-582.

Parker-Jenkins, M. (1993a) 'Muslim Rights', *Times Educational Supplement*, May 7, p.16.

Parker-Jenkins, M. (1993b) *Educating Muslim Children*, 2nd ed., Nottingham: School of Education.

Parker-Jenkins, M. (1994) 'Playing Fair with Muslims', *The Guardian*, November 8, p.8.

Parker-Jenkins, M. and Haw, K. (1995) (pending) 'The Educational Needs of Muslim Children in Britain: Accommodation or Neglect', in S. Vertovec (Ed) *Muslims, Europeans, Youth: Reproducing Ethnic and Religious Cultures*, London: Pluto Press.

Price, C. (1969) 'The Study of Assimilation', in J. A. Jackson (ed), *Migration*, Chicago: Chicago University Press, Sociological Studies No.2.

Pumfrey, P. D. and Verma, G. K. (1990) *Race Relations and Urban Education: Contexts and Promising Practices*, London: Falmer Press.

Qureshi, S. and Khan, J. (1989) *The Politics of Satanic Verses: Unmasking Western Attitudes*, Leicester: Muslim Communities Studies Institute.

The Holy Qur'an: English Translation of the Meanings and Commentaries, Madirah, Al-Munawarah; Saudi Arabia.

Rafferty, F. (1991) 'Muslim Boarding Schools Planned', *Times Educational Supplment*, 6 December, p.5.

Rahman, F. (1979) 2nd ed. *Islam*, Chicago: University of Chicago Press.

Rampton Committee (1981) *West Indian Children in our Schools*, Cmnd 8273. London: HMSO.

Rattansi, A. (1992) 'Changing the Subject? Racism, Culture and Education', in J. Donald and A. Rattansi (eds) *Race, Culture and Difference*, London: Sage Publications.

Raza, M. S. (1993) *Islam in Britain: Past, Present and Future*, Loughborough: Volcano Press Ltd., 2nd edition.

Reiss, M. (1993) 'What are the Aims of School Sex Education?', *Cambridge Journal of Education*, 23(2), pp.125-136.

Reynolds, D. (1984) (ed) *Studying School Effectiveness*, London: Falmer Press.

Robertson, A. H. (1982) *Human Rights in the World*, 2nd ed., Manchester: Manchester University Press.

Robinson, F. (1988) *Varieties of South Asian Islam*, Research Paper No.8, Centre for Ethnic Relations, University of Warwick.

Rushdie, S. (1988) *The Satanic Verses*, London: Viking.

Sanders, E. P. (1992) *Judaism: Practice and Belief*, London: SCM Press.

Sarwar, G. (1983) *Muslims and Education in the UK*, London: Muslim Educational Trust, 130 Stroud Green Road, London N4 3AZ.

Sarwar, G. (1989) *Sex Education: The Muslim Perspective*, London: Muslim Educational Trust, 130 Stroud Green Road, London N4 3AZ.

Sarwar, G. (1994) *British Muslims and Schools*, Muslim Educational Trust, 130 Stroud Green Road, London N4 3RZ.

Sarwar, G. (1992) *Islam Beliefs and Teachings* (4th ed), Muslim Educational Trust, 130 Stroud Green Road, London N43RZ.

Scarman, L. G. (1981) *Reports on the Inquiry into the Brixton Disorders*, London: HMSO, Cmnd 8427.

Siraj-Blatchford, I. (1993) 'Ethnicity and Conflict in Physical Education: a critique of Carroll and Hollinshead's case study', *British Educational Research Journal*, 19(1), pp.77-82.

Smith, G. (1990) 'The Next Ten Years', *Muslim Educational Quarterly*, 1(5), pp.26-27.

South Asian Development Partnership (1992) *South Asian Population for Great Britain*, Sutton, Surrey: SADP.

Spencer, D. (1990) 'Muslim girls await scarf ruling', *Times Educational Supplement*, 19 January, p.5.

Squelch, J. (1993) 'Education for Equality: The Challenge to Multicultural Education', in E. I. Dekker and E. M. Lemmer, *Critical Issues in Modern Education*, Durban: Butterworth Publishers (Pty) Ltd.

Steadman, J. (1984) 'Examination Results in Mixed and Single-Sex Schools', in D. Reynolds (ed) *Studying School Effectiveness*, London: Falmer Press.

The Sunday Times (1994) 'British Women Seek New Morality in Islam', Sept. 4, p.8.

Swann, M. (1985) *Education for All: A Summary of the Swann Report on the Education of Ethnic Minority Children*, Windsor: NFER- Nelson.

Taylor, M. and Hegarty, S. (1985) *The Best of Both Worlds ...? A Review of Research into the Education of Pupils of South Asian Origin*, Windsor: NFER-Nelson.

Tibawi, A. L. (1972) *Islamic Education*, London: Luzac.

Times (1993) 'Why British Women are Turning to Islam', 9 November, p.11.

Times Educational Supplement (1990) 'Parents Withdraw Pupils from Church of England Primary', 14 September, p.3.

Times Educational Supplement (1991) 'Warnock Backs Girls-Only State Sector', 1 March, p.10.

Times Educational Supplement (1994) 'Privateers Bring Taste of Monopoly', Sept. 2, p.8.

Tizard, B., Mortimore, J. and Burchell, B. (1988) 'Involving Parents from Minority Groups', in J. Bastiani (ed) *Parents and Teachers 2: From Policy to Practice*, London: NFER-Nelson.

Tomlinson, S. (1984) *Home and School in Multicultural Britain*, London: Batsford.

Tomlinson, S. (1990) *Multicultural Education in White Schools*, London: Batsford.

Tropp, A. (1957) *The School Teachers*, London: Heinemann.

Troyna, B. (1986) 'Beyond Multiculturalism: towards the enactment of anti-racist education in policy, provision and pedagogy', *Oxford Review of Education*, 13(3), pp.301-320.

Troyna, B. and Ball, W. (1987) *Views From the Chalkface*, (2nd ed), University of Warwick.

Troyna, B. and Selman, L. (1989) 'Surviving in the Survivalist Culture: anti-racist strategies and practice in the new ERA', in *The Journal of Further and Higher Education*, 13(2), Summer 1989, pp.22-36.

Troyna, B. and Williams, J. (1986) *Racism, Education and the State: the racialisation of education policy*, Beckenham: Croom Helm.

Trueba, H. T. (1989) *Raising Silent Voices*, New York: Harper- Collins Publishers Inc.

Turkish Daily News (1994) 'Religious 'Bias' in the West Against Islam', April 20, p.B3.

Union of Muslim Organisations (1976) *Guidelines and Syllabus on Islamic Education*, London: UMO.

Union of Muslim Organisations, Youth Council of UK and Eire, (1989) *Seminar on the Education Reform Act*, London: UMO.

Vassen, T. (1986) 'Curriculum Considerations in the Primary School', in J. Gundara et al, eds., *Racism, Diversity and Education*, London: Hodder and Stoughton.

Veasey, D. (1994) 'Sex Education: is its act together?', *Pastoral Care in Education*, 12(2), pp.13-22.

Vertovec, S. (ed) (1995) (pending) *Muslims, Europeans, Youth: Reproducing Ethnic and Religious Cultures*, London: Pluto Press.

The Voice (1994a) 'Boys Banned from School for being Rastas', March 22, p.4.

The Voice (1994b) 'School Head Re-writes Curriculum for her Pupils', April 26, p.3.

The Voice (1994) 'School Forced to Take Back Rasta Brothers', May 10, p.4.

The Voice (1994) 'Putting a Face to Our Past', p.10; and 'Setting the Record Straight', May 17, p.21.

The Voice (1994) 'Fascist Thug Guilty of Mob Savagery', June 14, p.5.

The Voice (1994) 'A Charter for Race Equality', June 14, p.7.

The Voice (1994) 'School Exclusion Scandal Continues', June 14, p.12.

The Voice (1994) 'Why Discipline is the Key to a Good Education', September 20, p.12.

Voll, J. O. (1991) 'Islamic Issues for Muslims in the United States', in Y. Y. Haddad, *Muslims in America*, Oxford: Oxford University Press.

Von Grunebaum, G. E. (1976) *Mohammedan Festivals*, London: Curzon.

Walford, G. (1994) 'The New Religious Grant-Maintained Schools', *Educational Management and Administration*, 22(2), pp.123-130.

Wardle, D. (1976) *English Popular Education 1780-1975*, 2nd ed. London: Cambridge University Press.

Watson, J. L. (1977) *Between Two Cultures: Migrants and Minorities in Britain*, *Oxford*: Basil Blackwell.

Weldon, F. (1989) *Sacred Cows*, London: Chatto and Windus.

Werbner, P. (1981) 'Manchester Pakistanis: Life Styles, Ritual and the Making of Social Distinctions', *New Community*, 9(2), pp.216-229.

Weston, C. (1989) 'Separate schools debate offers test', in *The Guardian*, July 22.

Wolfendale, S. (1992) *Empowering Parents and Teachers: Working for Children*, London: Cassell, pp.115.

Wood, A. (1960) *Nineteenth Century Britain*, London: Longmans.

Wright, C. (1992) *Race Relations in the Primary School*, London: David Fulton Publishers.

Yaseen, M. (1992) 'Charting New Directions', *Education*, 4 September, p.191.

Young, M. (1990) *Justice and the Politics of Difference*, Princeton, New Jersey: Princeton University Press.

Yuval-Davis, N. (1992) 'Fundamentalism, Multiculturalism and Women in Britain', in J. Donald and A. Rattansi (eds) *Race, Culture and Difference*, London: Sage Publications.

Appendix

Resources and Contacts

The following are contacts and resources to assist in teaching purposes. The list is by no means exhaustive but it indicates some of the resources available which teachers may find helpful.

The Muslim Educational Trust

Publishes a variety of books and teaching aids including:
i)   general publications on Islam;

ii)   subject specific issues eg. sex education and music education;

iii) audio-visual material.

Muslim Educational Trust
130 Stroud Green Road
London
N43 RZ

Iqra Trust

This organisation publishes a variety of books and booklets to provide information, guidance and clarification on Islamic matters:
i)   short booklets introducing Islam and Muslim practice;

ii)   children's library of books for 9-14 year olds;

iii) workcards on Science and Health Education etc.;

iv) classroom models relating to History, and Design Technology etc.;

v) materials for GCSE Islam.

Iqra Trust
24 Culross Street
London
WTY 3HE

Centre for the Study of Islam and Christian-Muslim Relations

Of particular interest are publications on Islam and Muslim communities in Europe.

CSIC
Selly Oak Colleges
Birmingham
B29 6LE

The Islamic Foundation

Publishes a variety of books on Islam for readers of all age groups, and produces audio-visual resources.

The Islamic Foundation Publications Unit
Unit 9, The Old Dunlop Factory
62 Evington Valley Road
Leicester LE5 5LJ

Islamic Educational Trust

Provides education, training, seminars, workpacks and publications on Islam.

Islamic Educational Trust
3-11 Keythorpe Street
Leicester

Indian Music Workshops

Workshops and tuition provided for schools and colleges on Indian music incorporating tabla vocals.

27 Crescent Road
Oxford
OX4 2NZ

Black Unicorn Books

Produces a variety of books on multiculturalism for children.

Black Unicorn Books
59 Cowley Road
The Plain
Oxford

Mobile Unit for Development Issues

MUNDI is an educational charity affiliated to the Development Education Association which offers a wide range of classroom materials on loan to schools. It provides resources, work packs, activities and posters on a variety of themes concerning multicultural education, many of which are designed to be used at various key stages within most National Curriculum subjects. Staff development and classroom activities also available.

MUNDI
School of Education
University of Nottingham
University Park
Nottingham

Muslim Information Services
233 Seven Sisters Road
London
N4 2DA

Islamic Video and Audio Centre
10 Hampden Road
London
NG 0H7

Halal Food Information

Is Your Diet Halal? A Guide to Halal and Haram Food Products (1993) This booklet was researched by the Muslim Food Board (UK) classifying some of the commonly available food products with information based on replies received from manufacturers. From:

The Islamic Centre, Leicester/The Muslim Food Board, UK
37 Hazelwood Road
Leicester LE5 5HR

What's In It For Me? (1991)
Produced by the Iqra Trust, this publication provides a guide to convenience and package foods, as well as fast food restaurants, identifying halal options:

Iqra Trust
24 Culcross Street
London
WTY 3HE

Bookshops

There are a variety of bookshops around the country which stock books on Islam and Islamic issues, such as:

Islamic Book Service
52 Fieldgate Street
London
E1 1DL

Islamic Book House
179 Anderton Road
Birmingham
B11 1NP

Islamic Book Centre
29 Hatherley Street
Liverpool
L8 2TJ

Islamic Book Centre
19 Carrington Street
Glasgow
GL 9AJ

Mirzan Books
141 Berridge Road
Forest Fields
Nottingham
NG7 6HR

Islamic Book Service
180 Belgrave
Middleway
Birmingham
B12 0XS

Index